THE CHRISTIAN INTELLECTUAL

THE CHRISTIAN INTELLECTUAL

by Jaroslav Pelikan

COLLINS
St James's Place, London
1966

This book first appeared as volume fourteen in the 'Religious Perspectives' series, edited by Ruth Nanda Anshen and published by Harper & Row, New York

Printed in Great Britain
by Cox & Wyman Limited,
London, Fakenham and Reading

Contents

Preface

The essays assembled in this volume are, in many ways, a counterpart to my recent study, *Obedient Rebels*. Like that book, *The Christian Intellectual* seeks, through historical research, to correlate Reformation thought with contemporary problems without doing violence to either. Although these chapters were written over the course of several years and, in earlier versions, for various purposes, they do have a unifying theme, which seems to suit them for publication in book form. For permission to reprint here material that originally appeared elsewhere, I am grateful to the American Philosophical Society, the University of Chicago Press and the University of Toronto Press.

JAROSLAV PELIKAN

Yale University
Holy Week, 1965

I
The Christian Intellectual on the Defensive

The Protestant Reformation was launched by a cadre of intellectuals, but the latter-day heirs of the Reformation sometimes seem determined to do everything they can to live down this past. Luther, Melanchthon, Bucer, Zwingli, Calvin, Cranmer, Hooker—all thought that they stood, as in fact they did, in the vanguard of the intellectuals of their time. Philip Melanchthon was speaking for an entire generation of biblical humanists and Reformers when he declared, in his inaugural address of August 29, 1518, at the University of Wittenberg: "With the Spirit as our guide and with the accompaniment of a cultivation of the liberal arts, we may then proceed to sacred studies. . . . In our hands we have Homer; we also have the Epistle of Paul to Titus."[1] Differ though they did among themselves both in their estimate of Homer and in their interpretation of the epistles of Paul, the "magisterial Reformers"[2] all spoke as colleagues, not as interlopers, when they addressed the architects of sixteenth-century culture.

The Christian intellectual of the twentieth century has no such sense of belonging. He is no longer in the vanguard, he is more often on the defensive. The essays assembled in this book all seek to provide some resources for a portrait of the Christian intellectual drawn on the basis of the thought of the

Reformation, especially that of Luther. But to put this portrait into relief we shall look first at the retreat of the Christian intellectual. It is, of course, not the Christian intellectual alone who is in retreat and on the defensive. The alienation between all intellectuals and their culture is a recurring theme of books published in recent years. Thus Max Hayward describes the poet of the Russian Revolution, Vladimir Majakovsky, as "one of those hypersensitive and introspective intellectuals for whom only total involvement in the turmoil and chaos of universal upheaval can offer any solution to hopeless inner agony." Paul Valéry suggested a parody of Descartes' *cogito* as the theme of the intellectual class: "This species complains; therefore it exists." James Reston observed in 1960 that "there has been a serious weakening of the ties between the men of ideas and the men of politics in this country during the last decade." Agreeing with him but extending the period of this alienation into earlier decades of American history as well, Hans J. Morgenthau has argued that "only when the intellectual is misunderstood or plays a popular act is he able to come to terms with society." In his study of one of the sources of the present situation, Andrew Sinclair has described how "the contempt of . . . young intellectuals of 1922 for their crass mother-country was replaced by their content [contempt] in 1938 for the efforts she was making to rescue herself and them." An apologist for the "new conservatism" has lamented "the emergence of a numerous class of . . . frivolous intellectuals" as "one of the least welcome phenomena of the age of modern capitalism. Their obtrusive stir repels discriminating people. They are a nuisance." David Riesman and Nathan Glazer have devoted a perceptive essay to the problem of "The Intellectuals and the Discontented Classes." And a minor character in a recent novel by John Gunther is referred to as "an intellectual, not one of the fighters."[3]

Nevertheless the alienation and retreat of the Christian

intellectual cannot be dismissed as simply one aspect of this general situation, for the Christian intellectual is on the defensive not only against other classes of society but against other intellectuals as well. At least since the Enlightenment, Christian intellectuals have been striving to recover that sense of dynamic involvement in contemporary thought which was so prominent in the work of the Reformation. Each successive movement of thought, from the rationalism of the eighteenth century to the existentialism of the twentieth, has evoked enthusiastic participation from Christian intellectuals, who have seen in it an opportunity for getting back into the mainstream of science, philosophy, and letters. Much of the history of modern theology, therefore, can be read as a series of apologetic efforts to seize that opportunity. But most historians of theology would probably agree with the judgment of Wilhelm Pauck that among such efforts "the product of the young Schleiermacher, *On Religion*, marks a turning point in the history of Christian theology. It represents the first creative effort on the part of a Christian thinker to interpret the Christian faith in relation to the 'modern' world-view. It shines forth in the splendor of a new discovery."[4] Schleiermacher's apology for religion, published at the end of the eighteenth century, documents graphically how a Christian intellectual and heir of the Reformation felt obliged to redefine his vocation as an apologist to modern culture.

The Apologist as Apostle

The vocation of the apologist is characterized by a sense of mission. He is concerned with "the cultured among [religion's] despisers," he speaks *ad gentes* or *contra gentiles* or *ad nationes.* Thus he partakes of the vocation of the apostle as one who has been sent and commissioned by Christ. The apologist knows himself to have received a charge from Another, and his apologetic assignment is in response and in fidelity to that charge. The nature of this charge may vary considerably within the limits of such fidelity, but one useful criterion for studying the vocation of any apologist is the question of what credentials he offers. In Schleiermacher's apologetics two sets of credentials appear, each of which helps to illumine the vocation of the apologist according to the *Addresses*.

At the very beginning of his appeal Schleiermacher presented one set of apostolic credentials, his certified membership in the class of those "who are experts [in religion], not only according to their own profession, but by recognition from the state and from the people." What would qualify him as an apostle according to these credentials would be his professional standing as a clergyman, attested to by the responsible spokesmen of society. But through most of *On Religion* this attestation was absent. When Schleiermacher did return to it, in the fourth address, he put himself on the side of the intellectuals whom he was addressing and decried the alliance of church and state, which certified as clergy many men who had not caught the spark of true religion. There were "many among the leaders of the church who understand nothing of religion, but who nevertheless, as servants of the state, are in a position to earn great official merit." It seems, then, that his preliminary appeal to the accreditation of the clergy by the state did not represent the basic credentials that Schleiermacher wanted to present to his audience.[5]

In the same breath with these credentials came a statement of the real grounds on which one Romantic intellectual claimed the right to speak to others, when he spoke of being "divinely swayed by an irresistible necessity within me . . . compelled to speak." At the beginning of the third address he likened this necessity to the creative urge that rises within the artist or musician, and he returned to this analogy in the fourth address.[6] From the lyrical, almost dithyrambic prose of these passages it is evident that for Schleiermacher himself this constituted his "impulse to write." He was responding to an impelling urge from within; this was his vocation, more than any mission from without.

For the purposes of this inquiry into the situation of the Christian intellectual, the significant feature of Schleiermacher's response to this inner necessity is that the secular intellectuals to whom he was speaking understood and revered such stirrings of the soul in the creative genius, even as they scorned the use of diplomas or pedigrees (and therefore of proof of ordination) to certify the poet or the wise man. The intellectuals to whom he addressed *On Religion* shared with him the conviction that an autonomous certification of the poet or wise man qualified him as no heteronomous validation of his education or lineage or orders could. By affirming this conviction Schleiermacher was attempting to show that the logic of the appeal from heteronomy to autonomy would support a further appeal from autonomy to theonomy. Thus the cultured were "however unintentionally, the rescuers and cherishers of religion,"[7] and Schleiermacher saw his apostolic mission in the discovery and documentation of their implicit piety.

Interpreted superficially, this undertaking might lend support to the equation of the vocation of the Christian intellectual with the pseudapostolate of the Gnostics. It seems to be a surrender of the objective warrant of the apostolic ministry to the free-floating subjectivity of the Romantic intellectual. If it is, and if the ministry of the Christian gospel needs such an objective warrant to be faithful to its apostolic vocation, then the vocation of the Christian apologist is indeed apostasy. But the ministry of Augustine and Chrysostom would suggest that the presentation of subjective credentials has always been a legitimate strategy in the announcement of the Christian message to the despisers—as well as to the devout. Indeed, the inclusion of Paul among the apostles represented an admission that such subjective credentials might have validity.[8] As for Schleiermacher himself, it can be argued that his "subjectivism," especially as it evolved into the theses of *The Christian Faith,* came to grasp some of the implications of the vocation of the apostle with unprecedented depth and acuteness.

The Apologist as Evangelist

The term "evangelist" as used here partakes of both meanings of the word: one who describes the meaning and message of Jesus Christ, as Matthew, Mark, Luke, and John did; and one who appeals to the unconverted to accept the meaning and message of Jesus Christ, as latter-day evangelists do. To assess the work of Schleiermacher the apologist, it is necessary to examine his message and to identify the appeal that he addressed to the cultured among the despisers of religion.

"The sum total of religion," Schleiermacher wrote, "is to feel that, in its highest unity, all that moves us in feeling is one; to feel that anything single and particular is possible only by means of this unity; to feel, that is to say, that our being and living is a being and living in and through God." This was his evangel, as he described to his readers what it meant to contemplate "the eternal existence of all finite things, in and through the Infinite, and of all temporal things in and through the Eternal." Throughout the second address he formulated his message in language almost reminiscent of physiology, speaking of "surrendering" and of "taking up into the inner unity of [one's] life and being" as, in a way, the metabolism of the religious life. In the name of such a conception of religion he gave an account that was at once empirical (in that he dealt with positive religion rather than with natural religion) and interpretive (in that he held no brief for the specific forms in which positive religion has appeared during history).[9]

A stress upon the positive religions set Schleiermacher off from most of the apologists of the century that was just coming to a close; it also made him an important figure in the beginnings of the scientific study of the history of religions that was about to begin. Some of the apologists of the eighteenth century had reduced the message of religion to God and immortality, with the possible addition of freedom; an older contemporary of Schleiermacher's had disposed of these issues two decades earlier in *The Critique of Pure Reason.* During the seventeenth century the apologists had concerned themselves with miracles, revelation, inspiration, and prophecies.[10] These issues had been producing "systems, commentaries, and apologies" during the sixteenth and seventeenth centuries, for in various combinations and with various concessions they had been identified as the content of religion. Now Schleiermacher was appealing to a higher court than reason, to *Gefühl.*[11] But the brief that he presented was not merely reason or feeling, but history.

"The spirit furnishes the chief nourishment for our piety, and history immediately and especially is for religion the richest source. History is of value for religion not because it hastens or controls in any way the progress of humanity in its development, but because it is the greatest and most general revelation of the deepest and holiest. In this sense, however, religion begins and ends with history." The message of religion, its evangel, must therefore always be a history as "the greatest and most general revelation." But that which was thus revealed was not general religion per se, just as the revelatory history was not just any history. The history that constituted the message was specific, but by means of it one could know the universal meaning of religion. Hence a preoccupation with "general religion" blinded the cultured despisers to the meaning of religious history; on the other hand, a preoccupation with the minutiae of religious history blinded the orthodox to the deepest meanings of the history, because they confused these minutiae with "the fundamental intuition of the religion."[12]

The message of this evangelist, therefore, was a sacred history, through which his hearers could learn the meaning of religion. What was the relation of this sacred history to the Christian evangel? The answer to that question may become clearer from an examination of Schleiermacher's performance in the second vocation of the evangelist as one who appeals and invites. As could be expected from his definition of religion, Schleiermacher would not insult his audience by bringing out the tired old proofs for the credibility of religion and the superiority of Christianity. Nor would he "recommend it merely as an accessory"[13] for keeping society moral. The history of such proofs supported the inner aversion both of the apologist and of his audience to this form of evangelism. If the apologist as evangelist was to make a bid for the loyalty of his intellectual readers, it had to be on other grounds.

One argument by which Schleiermacher appealed to the cultured despisers was the genetic. This is at least partly what he had in mind when he said in his peroration that his readers were "rooted with [their] whole knowing, doing, and being" in religion, specifically in Christianity. The genetic argument seemed to have particular force for him when he considered the preoccupation of both rationalism and Romanticism with moral issues. This preoccupation had given his readers a sense for teleology, which they mistakenly attributed to their ethics. Actually, Schleiermacher argued, such a teleology was a "torn off fragment" of religion rather than of morality. It could not have come into being without religion; and Schleiermacher, whose own mature ethic was to be rooted in his doctrine of the church, seems to have meant that this fragment could not be sustained without religion either.[14]

Nevertheless Schleiermacher's own ideas about the role of history in religion prevented any undue reliance upon the genetic argument. A more prominent appeal was the aesthetic.[15] One of the most powerful passages in the *Addresses* is that in which Schleiermacher challenged the intellectuals in his audience to consider the fuller implications of their fine-grained aesthetic sense, and thus from "the sight of a great and sublime work of art" to be "met by such a beam of your own sun and turned to religion." From this aesthetic realm came one of the metaphors in which the apologist cast his most basic appeal, an appeal that eventually transcended the aesthetic realm. "A man's special calling," he declared, "is the melody of his life, and it remains a simple, meager series of notes unless religion, with its endlessly rich variety, accompany it with all notes, and raise the simple song to a full-voiced, glorious harmony."[16] This would seem to be the most comprehensive of all his evangelistic appeals, for here he promised that the singular and individual perceptions which each man could identify as his own unique vocation were not negated but fulfilled by the coming of religion. On this ground both the genetic and the aesthetic evangel could make sense.

The Apologist as Prophet

If the apologist is to be heard, he must be able to speak the language of his hearers. But if he is to be worth hearing, he must differentiate himself sufficiently from his setting to stand over against it and to address it. The biblical office of the prophet illustrated this duality. The prophet was deeply rooted in the total life of Israel, including its political and cultic life—much more deeply rooted than the biblical scholarship of the nineteenth century acknowledged. At the same time, his commission from God obliged him to speak out against the people and also against the political and cultic life of Israel. Carrying out a prophetic office within his vocation as a Christian apologist, Schleiermacher had to direct his prophetic denunciation at two distinguishable (though not separable) entities, the organized church and the secular intelligentsia.

As has already been pointed out, Schleiermacher had deep

misgivings about the organized church, which reciprocated them. This meant, first of all, Roman Catholicism: "Modern Rome, godless but consistent, hurls anathemas and ejects heretics. Ancient Rome, truly pious and religious in a high style, was hospitable to every god." Eastern Orthodoxy, he believed, was practically "defunct"; for "all depth is lost in the mechanism of antiquated usages and liturgical forms." Anglicanism likewise was dead; "they know nothing of religion, except that they all preach devotion to ancient usages and defend its institutions." And so on through Christendom, as he summarized in one *ceterum censeo:* "Who would venture to say that all, that even the majority, that even the foremost and the most notable of those who for many a day have ruled the great ecclesiastical assembly, have been accomplished in religion or even members of the true church?"[17]

Nor were these merely the fulminations of an intellectual against the ecclesiastical activists. Some of the sharpest prophetic points were aimed at the theological intellectuals of the church, "who believe that the salvation of the world and the light of wisdom are to be found in a new vesture of formulas or in a new arrangement of ingenious proofs." Religion, he said, "is as far removed, by its whole nature, from all that is systematic as philosophy is naturally disposed to it"—this from the man who was to write the most important systematic theology since the *Institutes.* Even a cursory study of *The Christian Faith* will reveal how seriously Schleiermacher continued to take this Protestant principle even when he undertook the composition of a dogmatics. As his *Open Letter to Lücke* made evident, he applied to himself the principle he had voiced in *On Religion*: "[The theologian] is not only to be an inspired man and a teacher, but in humility he is to present himself also for universal testing. Nor shall anything be spared, not even what is most loved and dear; nor shall anything be indolently put aside, not even what is most generally acknowledged. Though it may be praised from without as something holy and may be set up before the world as the essence of religion, from within it must be subjected to a severe and repeated test."[18]

Because the prophet subjected himself and his church to a severe and repeated test, he had the right to speak a prophetic word to his culture as well. Schleiermacher the prophetic intellectual exercised that right to the limit. A quick catalogue of the vices he denounced will document both his power of observation and his courage. He saw the frustration of the do-gooders, who "wish to work on humanity . . . [and] have an ideal of the individual to which no one corresponds." In devastating language he described the precious spirits who "dart off into the great, glorious world to get for themselves little impressions: how they inspect the delicate markings and tints of flowers, or gaze at the magic play of colors in the glowing evening sky, and how they admire the songs of the birds on a beautiful countryside." With exquisite scorn he attacked the utilitarians, who had to be practical even about art and who used religion as an "occasion to win some few young people for caution and economy in the use of their powers and for the noble art of strengthening life."[19] These and other vices the prophetic apologist traced at least in part to the illiteracy about religion, any religion, that characterized the otherwise learned and sophisticated culture of the secular intellectuals to whom he was speaking.[20] In the power of his prophetic proclamation the apologist both identified himself with this culture and found the distance he needed to stand over against it and to address it.

The Apologist as Priest

The bête noire of the prophet is the priest. They have more in common than either of them would care to admit, and Schleiermacher's dogmatics brilliantly expounded the Christian intuition that saw prophet and priest converge in Christ

—but only there.[21] Of the two, it is clear that the priest stands in greater danger of capitulating to his culture. Because his is a ministry of mediation, the priest tends to substitute "both/and" for "either/or." How an apologist understands his priestly ministry of mediation, therefore, is a useful guide to understanding his vocation.

"As a man I speak to you of the sacred mysteries of mankind according to my view, of what was within me when with youthful enthusiasm I sought the unknown, of what since then I have thought and experienced, of the innermost springs of my being which shall forever remain for me the highest." In this celebrated strophe at the beginning of the *Addresses* Schleiermacher announced his priestly commission to initiate his readers into the sacred mysteries. Later he spoke again of "sacred mysteries discovered and solemnized, which are not mere insignificant symbols but, rightly considered, are natural indications of a certain kind of consciousness and of certain feelings." Repeatedly he described his apologetic vocation as that of mediating between religion and the scornful intellectuals of the time. That was indeed the vocation of the seers and saints, who mediated "between your limited way of thinking and the eternal laws of the world." It seems that Schleiermacher the apologist saw himself as a priest inducting the mystes into the holy place, but acknowledged that others or Another had to act as high priest.[22]

Some such distinction between priest and high priest would seem necessary to treat fairly and accurately the role of Christendom as mediator between mankind and the sacred mysteries of mankind. This was the role that Schleiermacher envisaged for the empirical church, standing as it did between the world and the true church. It was to be, he said, "a mediating institution whereby to come into a certain contact with [the true church], as it were an atmosphere, both as a medium for purification and to attract new material." Here he anticipated the reinterpretation of the priesthood of believers that he was to formulate later: "Christendom as a whole, as the human race already united to the Redeemer, stands to the rest of humanity in the relation in which the priests stood to the laity. For it is only in so far as there exists a real vital fellowship with Christ at least in one part of the race that there is also a relationship between him and the rest."[23]

It would therefore be bearing false witness to represent this Christian intellectual as a self-anointed priest who usurped a mediatorial vocation between the church and the world. His awareness of the spots and wrinkles in empirical Christendom did sometimes outweigh his institutional loyalty; but outweighing both was his conviction that through the mediation of empirical Christendom, with all its spots and wrinkles, it was nevertheless possible for men to be reconciled with the Infinite. Accompanying this realism about the church visible, however, was a sense of being set apart from the common masses, and therefore also from the church. Consideration of the apologist's vocation as priest must raise the question whether the identification of the Christian intellectual with his culture has also allied him with other intellctuals more closely than he is allied with other Christians. In other words, apologetics must deal with the problem called accommodationism in the history of missions.

There is much evidence to support the contention that the Christian intellectual who wrote *On Religion* felt closer to other intellectuals than to other Christians. He was proud that his speech did not betray his ministerial office—"betray" in the sense of "tip off"! He could contrast "the people" with "all who want to be considered cultured." He spoke of "our party." The conventional religionists "do not despise religion, and they are not to be called cultured. But they destroy religion as much as they can. . . . They are still the dominating party, and you and we are but a very few." He was sometimes so snobbish and condescending as to be priggish in his treatment of "the commonest forms of humanity, ever returning in a thousand copies." When he spoke of "descending among persons limited to one earthly aim and effort . . . a steward of religion among unbelievers, a missionary among savages . . . an Orpheus or Amphion . . . a priestly figure," he was speaking both as a priest of the sacred mysteries of Christ and as a member of an intellectual elite. Apparently Schleiermacher sensed the danger in this confusion. Therefore he immediately took pains, in the very next paragraph, to clarify his affinity for, but also his differentiation from, the secular intellectuals.[24]

The Apologist as Disciple

The evangelist calls others as one who has himself been called. Similarly, the disciple teaches others as one who has himself been taught. A theological evaluation of the vocation of the Christian apologist must pay attention, therefore, not only to what and how he teaches but also to how he interprets his having been taught. Hence the vocation of the apologist must be interpreted within the framework of the relation between master and disciple.

The language in which Schleiermacher described the dependence of disciple upon master stressed the maieutic and temporary role of the master. In religion, "if anywhere, this tutelage is only a passing state. Hereafter, each man shall see with his own eyes, and shall produce some contribution to the treasures of religion. . . . You are right in despising the wretched echoes who derive their religion entirely from another." Perhaps the most significant statement of his view came in the third address: "Of course there is in religion a mastership and a discipleship. But this attachment is no blind imitation. It is not the master that makes disciples, but he is their master because of their choice." A later note appended to this passage was an effort to square it with the biblical view of election. Yet Schleiermacher could not extricate himself from the implications of his position on the meaning of discipleship. "It is most preposterous," he said, "to wish to limit any pupil to a single master." He was even willing to posit a Platonic doctrine of recollection in support of this view of disciple and master.[25]

From some of these passages it might appear that Schleiermacher, like Kierkegaard and Augustine, was operating with a qualitative distinction between human teachers and Christ as teacher. Then discipleship to Christ would be different in kind from discipleship to any other master. Whether or not this was his later and more mature position, it seems clear that he intended no such distinction here. In fact, each time he referred to Christ he immediately explained that he was not making this distinction. Speaking of "one of the greatest heroes of religion" whose observation of the lilies of the field had given him serenity, Schleiermacher immediately went on to say: "How much more should we gain [insight and serenity], we who have been permitted by a richer age to go deeper!" In the most extensive reference to Christ anywhere in the *Addresses*, the same warning appeared: "Yet he never maintained that he was the only mediator, the only one in whom his idea had actualized itself. All who attach themselves to him and who form his church should also be mediators with him and through him."[26] This seems to show that the general axioms regarding master and disciple quoted earlier applied also to the relation between Christ and the Christian.

Yet it would be inadequate and unfair to leave the problem of discipleship here. There was one more element in Schleiermacher's handling of the problem that qualified and deepened his view of it. This was his recognition of the subtle connection between discipleship and individuality. His polemic was directed against both an individualistic and a slavish distortion of that connection. In one of his most penetrating discussions he set out to show that when several persons refer their personal religion to the same relation and call this relation the source of their devotion, this does not necessarily mean that they have surrendered their individuality to one another or to the source. "Thus understood," he said a little later, "the church is properly called the common mother of us all." Discipleship meant the recovery of authentic selfhood in relation to other disciples. It meant also the growth of the disciple from the status of servant to the status of brother and friend in relation to Christ the master.[27]

The Apologist as Betrayer

Critics of the apologetic enterprise within the church have often pointed out that the Christian intellectuals who have courted the enemies of Christ have thereby put themselves into the tradition of Judas Iscariot, the betrayer. Schleiermacher has been accused of compounded treason; as he pointed out years later, it was difficult to understand how he could have been guilty of all these mutually contradictory betrayals at the same time. He has repeatedly been accused of betraying the cause of the institutional church to its Romantic critics. His opponents charged him with betraying theology to the speculations of "the holy, rejected Spinoza" and "the divine Plato." Some readers saw his willingness to put the Bible on the plane of "every later utterance of the whole church, and therefore of the Divine Spirit" as a betrayal of Protestantism to Roman Catholicism. The Romantics, meanwhile, felt betrayed by his curious stubbornness about remaining a theologian, a clergyman, and even a preacher, when some of the best minds of the time were moving from theology to history and philosophy.[28]

But the fundamental betrayal of which Schleiermacher has been accused is the betrayal of Christian revelation to the *Gefühl* of the natural man. Revelation became "every original and new communication of the universe to man." Grace was equated with "interchange between the entrance of the world into man, through intuition and feeling, and the outgoing of man into the world, through action and culture." The Christian message speaks about a point in time; but (to stay with the mathematical metaphor) "the whole circumference of religion is infinite, and is not to be comprehended under one form, but only under the sum total of all forms." The doctrine of the incarnation is a way of speaking about a particular man and a particular event under Pontius Pilate, but Schleiermacher could say at the beginning of his last address: "I would, as it were, conduct you to the God that has become flesh. . . . I would have you discover religion in the religions." And if none of these religions could provide a man with a spiritual home, he was not to feel restrained "from developing a religion suitable to his own nature and his own religious sense."[29]

Thus the Christian intellectual jeopardized both his relation to the church and his participation in the life of culture when he sought to address essays on religion to the cultured among its despisers. As Karl Barth has said: "It will not do to lodge a complaint against Schleiermacher that, because in every conflict he always accepted the opinion of the culture and denied the opinion of traditional Christianity, he consciously betrayed Christianity to the learning and the cultural consciousness of his time. But if one is to avoid this complaint—and avoid it we must—then there is no alternative but the recognition that as an apologist for Christianity he truly played upon it as a virtuoso plays upon his violin, [selecting] those tones and melodies that would sound, if not pleasant, then at least acceptable to his hearers. Schleiermacher speaks not as a responsible servant, but, in true virtuoso fashion, as a free master of this material."[30] But such an "apologetic by abdication," which is able to speak to its culture only by reducing the content of its message, seems doomed to failure; for it will remove layer after layer of its tradition, in response to one objection or another, until there is no significant continuity left between it and the evangel in whose name it claims to speak.

In the chapters that follow we shall examine the Christian thought of the Reformation with a view toward discovering both some of its affinities with modern thought and some of the characteristics that make it unacceptable or even unintelligible to the modern intellectual; for both are present, particularly in those ideas of the Reformers which the Christian intellectual of the twentieth century finds most appealing. These essays, therefore, will sometimes seem to oscillate between the sixteenth century and modern thought, but the Christian thought of Luther's Reformation is the primary focus of their attention. Another Christian intellectual from the sixteenth century, Francis Bacon, in his *Advancement of Learning,* proposed a distinction between "three knowledges: divine philosophy, natural philosophy, and human philosophy or humanity."[31] This distinction can serve as a basis for our Reformation portrait of the Christian intellectual. We have treated the theology or "divine philosophy" of Luther's Reformation in *Obedient Rebels,* but even that study began and ended with consideration of the latter two "knowledges" in Bacon's scheme.[32] The present volume will deal, in turn, with "natural philosophy" and with "the humanities."

Part One

Christian Thought and Natural Philosophy

II
The Challenge to Creation

While Schleiermacher was attempting to redefine the vocation of the Christian intellectual in relation to Romanticism at the end of the eighteenth century, preliminary skirmishes were already being fought in the conflict that was to do more than any other to put the Christian intellectual on the defensive: the challenge to the Christian doctrine of creation that came from natural philosophy, in the form of the discovery of biological evolution. Schleiermacher himself was aware of the challenge, as his dogmatic work showed.[1] But in 1834, the year Schleiermacher died, Charles Darwin had finished only half of the cruise of "The Beagle," which led to the publication in 1859 of his *Origin of Species.*

The Sources of the Conflict

Seldom in the history of the Christian church have theologians reacted as violently to a nontheological book as they did to Charles Darwin's *Origin of Species.* Neither the *True Word* of Celsus nor *The Revolutions of the Heavenly Bodies* of Copernicus nor even perhaps *The Communist Manifesto,* damaging though they all were to the cherished beliefs of many Christians, did so much to dramatize the alienation of the Christian intellectual from the world of thought around him. Clearly Darwinism seemed to be a challenge to something central in Christian faith and life. Bishop Wilberforce and William Jennings Bryan are partly illustrations and partly caricatures of a defensiveness that pervaded Christian thought during the two generations following the *Origin of Species.*

How are we to explain that defensiveness? Even if the answer confines itself to the area of Christian doctrine and ignores the important psychological, sociological, and cultural factors in the life of the church that help to account for its defensive stance,[2] the explanation is not as obvious as either Thomas Huxley and Clarence Darrow or Samuel Wilberforce and William Jennings Bryan thought it was. For diverse and even divergent ideas within the broad Christian tradition found themselves threatened by the doctrine of organic evolution. In the opinion of many theologians Darwin threatened the trustworthiness of the Scriptures by casting doubt upon the literal accuracy of the narratives in the book of Genesis; but Copernicus had also been accused of subverting the truth of the Bible.[3] The traditional Christian definition of the image of God in man seemed to clash with the idea of his descent from earlier and lower forms of life, but the voyages of discovery and the beginnings of modern cosmography had already shaken some of the foundations of the classical Christian interpretation of the image of God.[4] Faith in the direction of divine providence over nature, as formulated by writers like William Paley in his *Natural Theology,* could not stand if Darwin was right; but the orthodox rationalism which Paley both attacked and shared had already substituted its own doctrines of historical destiny for the orthodox, largely Augustinian concept of divine providence.[5] Darwin's suggestions about the descent of man appeared to make the Augustinian doctrine of original sin through the fall of one human couple untenable, but so did the various versions of the idea of preadamites that had achieved some currency during the seventeenth and eighteenth centuries.[6]

All these Christian doctrines, and many others besides,

seemed to lose their moorings when Darwin cut the rope between man and Adam. One or another of them predominated in the reactions of various Christian intellectuals to the Darwinian hypothesis. Yet the one fundamental Christian doctrine to which Darwin seemed to pose the most direct challenge was certainly the doctrine of creation. If evolution was right, creation was wrong: on this premise, it appears, Huxley and Wilberforce, Bryan and Darrow were all in agreement. Because that premise was supported by so heterogeneous a community of scholars and orators on both sides, it seems to deserve some special examination in our study of the predicament of the Christian intellectual. From a study of the history of the doctrine of creation it is clear that by the nineteenth century Christian thought had come to emphasize those aspects of biblical and patristic language to which Darwinism represented a challenge; and it had meanwhile tended to ignore, or rather to neglect, those aspects of the patristic and Reformation traditions which theology could maintain even in the face of scientific discoveries about the origin of species and the descent of man. There is, unfortunately, no full-length history of the Christian doctrine of creation.[7] One issue which any such history would have to study is the ambiguity in the very term "creation" which has been present throughout both Jewish and Christian history.

Creation in the Bible

Although the story of how God originally fashioned the world and all that is in it comes first in the sequence of the biblical narratives as we now have them, it is a mistake to interpret this story as the foundation for all the subsequent narratives. Indeed, literary analysis of the creation stories suggests that they come rather late in the history of the development of the Old Testament.[8] Both on the basis of such analysis and from historical examination it seems clear, in the apt formulation of

Werner Foerster, "that the primary witness of the Old Testament is [the witness] to the God who is sovereign over history, the God of Abraham, Isaac, and Jacob, the God who led the people of Israel out of Egypt through the Red Sea and the Jordan into the Promised Land, the God who directed the wars of Israel. The sequence in the Old Testament is not from creation to history, but vice versa. Thus it is not: 'The Creator (subject) is Jahweh (i.e., the God of Israel)'; but rather 'Jahweh (subject) is the Creator.' "[9] Therefore the story or stories of creation in Genesis are not chiefly cosmogony, but the preface to the history that begins with the calling of Abraham. Genesis is not world history, but the history of the covenant people of God. And as the book of Exodus spoke of Pharaoh only for the sake of his part in the exodus of Israel and otherwise cared so little about him that the Pharaoh of the exodus is still difficult to identify historically, so the book of Genesis was interested in "the heavens and the earth" as the stage for the essentially historical rather than cosmic drama it set out to recount.

The vocabulary of the Bible bears out this literary and theological conclusion.[10] The verb used for "create" in the first verse of the Bible is *bara*. The same verb is used to designate the sovereign action of God in history in other passages of the Pentateuch (e.g., Ex. 34 : 10, Num. 16 : 30)—passages which perhaps constitute the earliest instances of *bara* in biblical Hebrew. All instances of the verb support this generalization: *bara* always has God as its subject, never creatures. The same is true of *ktizein*, the verb used by the New Testament to translate *bara*. Sometimes *ktizein* refers to the original constitution of the world; sometimes it refers to an action of God in history, especially to the coming of Christ as the "new creation." But always it refers to an action whose ultimate actor is God, though the action may take place through created agents. Thus the central meaning of the biblical words for "create" is divine activity, regardless of when the "creating" is said to have taken place or how or from what previously existing materials, if any. The most common verb for "create" in the Old Testament is not *bara* at all, but *asah;* and although it may refer also to what men "make" or "do," it is employed both for God's "making" in the beginning and for his "making" in the processes of history, particularly of Israel's history.

Whatever the Genesis stories mean by "creation," therefore, must be, first, part of what the Bible means by the God of the covenant and, secondly, part of how the Bible looks at the meaning of the present, empirical world. The "God" who is the subject of the verb "create" is the God of Abraham, Isaac, and Jacob in the Old Testament, the Father of Christ in the New. The "world" which is the object of the verb "create" is the world in which Israel lives now as a creature of that God. Creation, therefore, is not principally an account of origins but of dependence. It is not intended to say primarily how things began but how they are in relation to God. The most characteristic view of creation in the Old Testament is not the story in Genesis 1–3 but Psalm 104: "Thou dost cause the grass to grow for the cattle, and plants for man to cultivate, that he may bring forth food from the earth, and wine to gladden the heart of man, oil to make his face shine, and bread to strengthen man's heart. These all look to thee, to give them their food in due season. When thou givest to them, they gather it up; when thou openest thy hand, they are filled with good things. When thou hidest thy face, they are dismayed; when thou takest away their breath, they die and return to their dust. When thou sendest forth thy Spirit, they are created; and thou renewest the face of the ground." The Psalmist knows that man must cultivate the earth and squeeze the grape, but he looks with thanksgiving and reverence to the God of the covenant who is at work creating here and now through these very means. As chapter five will point out, the most profound biblical statement of this theme is Psalm 139.

From this insight, which Israel claimed to have received by divine self-disclosure about the ways of God in history, it necessarily followed that neither nature nor history had ever been without the presence of the divine activity, and that therefore God was also the initiator of both nature and human history. Thus it is that the stories of creation take their place in the biblical witness to the ways of God. The sun would not smite by day, nor the moon by night, because the God of the covenant was ultimately trustworthy and had always been so. The story of the creation in six days and the story of Adam and Eve both belong to the history of how God deals with those to whom he has bound himself by a covenant and a law. Hence the origin of the universe and the origin of man are both predicated of the God whom Israel has come to know, through covenant and law, as the God of mercy and of justice. To the New Testament this applies, if anything, with even greater force; for here creation, in so far as it receives any attention at all, is presupposed on the basis of the Old Testament, ascribed to the God and Father of our Lord Jesus Christ, and correlated with redemption.[11] Only seldom in either the Old or the New Testament is the Genesis story referred to as a causal explanation for man's dependence upon his Creator now. More often it is read as an account of what goes on every day.[12]

Beginnings of Apologetics

Because the New Testament presupposed creation on the basis of the Old Testament, there was no controversy about creation so long as Christianity remained part of Judaism. But soon after it ventured forth into the Hellenistic Roman world, it found itself obliged to defend the doctrine of creation. Both of the apologetic sermons in the book of Acts (Acts 14 : 15; 17 : 24–28) quote Paul as taking up the defense of creation when he addressed the "cultured despisers" of Christianity.

Significantly, in both sermons he is represented as defending the original creation and the continuing creation simultaneously. Justin Martyr, mingling quotations from Plato with the Scriptures, was willing to define creation as the shaping of a matter that was already in existence. Against the enemies of the faith Justin therefore defended the rationality of the notion that God was the Creator in this sense of the word.[13] The earliest known apology for Christianity, that of Aristides, declared—according to a very late and rather dubious recension of its text—that God is "the one who arranged all things and pervades them" (*ton systesamenon ta panta kai diakratounta*).[14] This appears to adumbrate the later distinction between the original creation and the continuing preservation of the world. The Syrian church father Tatian, who proved to be a heretic (though on other grounds), wrote that God had first called matter into being and then had fashioned the world from this pre-existent, albeit created, stuff.[15] Other fathers—for example, Clement of Alexandria—tried various related explanations of the relation between the creating activity of God and matter.[16]

Apparently the first church father to assert clearly that creation was *creatio ex nihilo* was Theophilus of Antioch. He writes that "they [the prophets] taught us with one consent that God made all things out of nothing; for nothing was coaeval with God: but he being his own place, and wanting nothing, and existing before the ages, willed to make man by whom he might be known; for him, therefore, he prepared the world."[17] Now the doctrine of *creatio ex nihilo* may be implied in the writings of the prophets, as Theophilus claims. But apart from the Apocrypha it is taught explicitly in only two places in the Bible, both of them in the New Testament (Rom. 4 : 17; Heb. 11 : 3). Neither of these places uses the technical term for "create," *ktizein;* on the other hand, all instances of *ktizein* appear to ignore the issue of *creatio ex nihilo*. Theophilus finds it a necessary corollary to the biblical understanding of creation and sets it forth as such. Even he goes on to say a little later that "matter, from which God made and fashioned the world, was in some manner created, being produced by God." Faced by the doctrine of certain Greeks that the world, or perhaps matter, was coeternal with God and that God was therefore dependent upon the world, Theophilus declared *creatio ex nihilo* as proof that the dependency in the relation between God and the world was all in one direction. So began the identification of creation primarily or exclusively with *creatio ex nihilo,* which crowded continuing creation out of the attention of the theologians.

The identification became even more explicit in the man who shaped much of the theological vocabulary of the Latin-speaking Christian West, Tertullian. His *Treatise Against Hermogenes* is a full-scale refutation of the claim that matter existed before creation. Creation must mean *creatio ex nihilo,* even though the creation accounts do not say this in so many words: "If God could make all things out of nothing, Scripture could quite well omit to add that he had made them out of nothing, but it should have said by all means that he had made them out of matter, if he had done so; for the first possibility would be completely understandable, even if it was not expressly stated, but the second would be doubtful, unless it were stated."[18] In the argumentation of Theophilus and Tertullian—and later on, as we shall see, in the argumentation of Thomas Aquinas—the polemical target of the *creatio ex nihilo* was one or another Greek doctrine about the eternity of the world. The implication of this doctrine for the Christian war against Greek ideas helped theologians like Tertullian to make the doctrine of creation primarily, though never exclusively, a question of origins.

What helped to save Tertullian from making creation exclusively a question of origins *ex nihilo* was his war against Gnostic ideas, as represented by Marcion. A deep aversion for the created world of matter caused Marcion and the Gnostics to separate God the Creator from God the Redeemer. Marcion taught that these were two separate gods. The Creator, of whom the Old Testament speaks, was inferior to the Father of our Lord Jesus Christ. Tertullian quotes the Marcionites as saying: "Our God, although he did not manifest himself from the beginning and by means of the creation, has yet revealed himself in Christ Jesus."[19] Thus Gnosticism taught a radical discontinuity between salvation and creation, including in this latter term the present empirical world of matter. Consistently carried out, such a doctrine of discontinuity would have pushed the idea of creation so far back into history and so far down into matter that the spiritual-minded Gnostic would not have to soil himself with creation at all. In their answer to this denigration of creation Tertullian and the other anti-Gnostic fathers asserted the identity of the Creator with the Father of Christ. Christ "entered on his ministry with the very attributes of the Creator."[20] Therefore the God who acts in history is the Creator: this fundamental conviction of Israel's faith found an echo in the church's faith as patristic theology defended the faith against Gnosticism. Nevertheless, the root meaning of "creation" was now *creatio ex nihilo.*

The Thomistic Definition

In the various summaries of the church's faith and of patristic theology that root meaning took precedence. When the most masterful of these summaries came to be composed in the thirteenth century, Christianity was once more contending with the doctrine of the eternity of the world, revived for it by the skepticism of the Averroists and by the rediscovery of the physical writings of Aristotle. Seeing in Aristotle the most complete documentation of what the unaided human mind was able to discover about God, man, and the world, Thomas Aquinas refused to attempt what some of the church fathers had attempted. Instead of trying to prove from reason that the world was a product of divine creation and not coeternal with God, Thomas declared that this doctrine, like the doctrine of the divine Trinity, was a matter not of reason but of revelation.[21] The dependence of the present empirical world upon God, on the other hand, was part of the system of motions and causes that underlay his celebrated "five ways"; and thus it belonged to natural theology, not merely to revealed theology.[22] Here once more the polemical situation compelled a theologian to stress original creation more than continuing creation and to make creation chiefly a matter of beginnings rather than of dependence.

So one-sided was this stress that Thomas found it difficult to apply the word "create" to anything except the original creation at the beginning. He quotes Augustine as saying that "to make concerns what did not exist at all, but to create is to make something by bringing it forth from what was already existing." To this quotation Thomas opposes the authority of the *Glossa ordinaria,* which comments upon Genesis 1 : 1 with the definition: "To create is to make something from nothing." Accepting the definition of the *Glossa,* Thomas concludes: "Augustine uses the term 'creation' in an equivocal sense, according as to be created signified improvement in things; as when we say that a bishop is created. This is not the way in which we here use the term creation, but in the way already stated," namely, as *creatio ex nihilo.*[23] In the conflict over creation and in the clarification of what creation meant, continuing creation was not at issue, but original creation was. Thus it could be concluded either that continuing creation was dependent for its validation upon the assertion of original creation, or that the two were quite separate; whichever of these conclusions was accepted, the connection between the two, which had been characteristic of earlier Christian thought and language, was less prominent than the distinction between them. At the same time, the Thomistic theory of essence and existence provided a framework within which both original creation and continuing creation could be formulated.[24]

Creation in Reformation Thought

Although the Protestant Reformers did not articulate their theories of essence and existence as precisely as Thomas had, they retained the traditional understanding of creation. Thus for Luther, God's "resting" on the seventh day meant "that God ceased in such a way that he did not create another heaven and another earth. It does not denote that God gave up preserving and governing the heaven and the earth which had already been created. . . . He has, therefore, ceased to establish; but he has not ceased to govern."[25] In his preaching and in his catechisms Luther spoke about the continuing creation, as did Calvin; but if there is any difference between the Reformers and their scholastic predecessors over the doctrine of creation, it is only of emphasis, because of the more existentialist cast of Reformation thought.[26] The distinction between creation and preservation, as well as the continuity between them, survived the Reformation and became a standard part of the vocabulary employed by the codifiers of Reformation thought in the Protestant Orthodoxy of the seventeenth century. One of these codifiers, Johann Andreas Quenstedt, summarized the continuity this way: "God preserves all things through a continuation of the action by which he originally produced things. For the preservation of a thing is, strictly speaking, nothing else than the continuing production of it; nor do they [creation and preservation] differ except in their outward designation" (*per extrinsecam quandam denominationem*).[27]

It was not, however, through its emphasis upon continuing creation that the Protestant Reformation helped to shape the doctrine of creation, but through its emphasis upon history, specifically through its insistence upon the unrepeatable character of events in the history of God's dealing with man. The immediate occasion for this insistence was the form which the interpretation of the Mass had sometimes taken in the later Middle Ages. Folk piety said unreflectively–and learned medieval theology said more carefully, though often not very much more carefully–that the sacrifice of Christ on Calvary was repeated every day in the unbloody sacrifice of the Mass. Even after the Council of Trent and the theologians who expounded the decrees of the Council had introduced far greater precision and restraint into Roman Catholic language about the repeated sacrifice, Protestant theology continued to regard such language as a fundamental distortion of the New Testament gospel. Protestant theology therefore fastened upon the biblical declarations that what Christ had done was "once and for all" (*ephapax*). Therefore the sacrifice on Calvary neither could nor should be repeated in the Mass.[28]

For the purposes of our study of the Reformation the controversy over the "once and for all" is important because of the parallel that could so easily be drawn between redemption and creation. God was always the Redeemer; but he was this on the ground of an unrepeatable historical event, the life, death, and resurrection of Jesus Christ. Since Adam was a type of Christ, the conclusion was readily available: God was always the Creator; but he was this on the ground of an unrepeatable historical event, the creation of the universe *ex nihilo* at a specific time in the not too distant past and the formation of the first human pair from the dust of the earth. *Einmaligkeit,* "unrepeatability," was thus predicated of creation in analogy to redemption. To dispute the historicity of Jesus Christ meant to undermine faith in the unrepeatable redemption of the human race, which had taken place between 1 and 33 A.D. By analogy, to question the historicity of Adam and Eve meant to subvert the Christian doctrine of the unrepeatable creation of the human race. We must turn next, therefore, to a study of the irony in the Reformation view of creation. For, as we noted at the beginning of chapter one, the Reformers claimed that their "historical" exegesis of the Bible made them part of the revival of knowledge in the sixteenth century. Yet this very exegesis also made some Christian intellectuals who stood in the tradition of the Reformers unable to cope with the revival of knowledge in the nineteenth and twentieth centuries.

III
Creation as History

The most massive achievement of Luther's intellectual work were his *Lectures on Genesis,* which occupied him from 1535 to 1545.[1] Although his principal concern in these lectures was with "the history of the people of God,"[2] the two creation narratives at the very beginning of the book of Genesis and the story of the deluge a little later did compel him to give the problem of creation as history more sustained attention than he did anywhere else in his works. The manuscript of his lectures has been bowdlerized by his more orthodox disciples, who were in many ways closer to Melanchthon than to Luther; but for the purposes of this study their editorial corrections provide further evidence of the predicament of the Christian intellectual in Reformation and post-Reformation history.[3]

The Historical Sense

When Luther took up the exposition of Genesis, he knew that he was following a long succession of exegetes from both the patristic and medieval period who had commented upon it before him. From the vast majority of these he set himself consciously apart, on the grounds that his exegesis of the text was strictly historical while that of the tradition had been unduly preoccupied with allegories. It was "the historical and strict meaning" of the text that he strove to discover, "the historical and literal meaning, which is in harmony with the text." He read the accounts of the book of Genesis as history, postponing allegorical interpretation until he had determined the historical sense. For allegory was to this historical sense what rhetoric was to logic; "it ought to illustrate the historical account but has no value at all for giving proof." As the natural color of a body surpassed even a beautiful painting, so the historical interpretation of a passage surpassed the allegorical interpretation.[4]

Both Luther the Reformer and Luther the intellectual were speaking here. The recovery of the historical sense of the Scriptures was a requirement both of his theology and of his scholarship. As one of the first theologians since the ancient church to study the Old Testament in the original Hebrew, Luther made use of the best textual, lexicographical, and historical data available to him in the scholarship of men like Johannes Reuchlin, Santes Pagninus, and (through the Franciscan Nicolaus of Lyra) the medieval rabbis. Some of his textual conjectures and linguistic intuitions were exceedingly acute and have been substantiated by later research.[5] Yet he was also critical of an exegesis that neglected theology for the sake of mere philology; such an exegesis failed to grasp the historical meaning of the text.[6] When Moses spoke of six days, he must have meant six literal days. It is ironic that whereas later theologians tried to accommodate their exegesis to science by extending the six days to six epochs, Luther was concerned with the opposite extreme; he was attacking theologians like Augustine and Hilary, in whose exegesis the hexaemeron was reduced to a single instantaneous act of creation. For Luther, such exegesis was sophistry. He was so bent upon historical interpretation, in the name of both scholarship and faith, that he tried to gauge the time of day when Eve was tempted and fell, deciding that it was at noon.[7]

The State of Innocence

Applied to the narrative of the first three chapters of the book of Genesis, this insistence upon the historical meaning of the text compelled Luther to treat the account of the state of innocence as narrative prose. Repeatedly he confessed how difficult such an interpretation was—not because of the absurdities to which it led, but because "we cannot even conceive of it [the *status integritatis*] in our thinking." "Now that we have lost the state of living in innocence," he complained, "it is easier to form an opinion about that life than to give an actual description of it."[8] But he did form many opinions about it and did try to give as detailed and accurate a description of it as he could. He puzzled over the problem of the sanitary facilities in the menagerie on Noah's ark; and instead of asking the hackneyed question of where Cain found his wife, Luther expressed his admiration for a girl who would marry—or remained married to—a man guilty of so heinous a crime.[9] As a spokesman for the new learning, then, Luther set forth an exegesis destined to be shaken by each successive stage of scientific discovery about both man and the world. Columbus supposed that on his third voyage he had discovered earthly Paradise; thus "mythical geography still obsessed the man who had just opened up the way to so many real discoveries."[10] In the same fashion Martin Luther, who effected a "Copernican revolution"[11] in Christian theology, was still obsessed by the vision of a historical state of integrity, in which both man and the world lived as the will of the Creator had originally intended them to live before the fall into sin.

This obsession with a historical fall required Luther to use exaggerated language about the purity and nobility of man in the state of innocence. He had to say that the physical prowess of man then exceeded anything possible now. If man had not fallen into sin, children would not have needed to be nursed by their mothers for very long. In fact, they would have been able to stand upright immediately, as baby chicks do, and to run about. Childbirth would have been without pain, and the fertility of the human female would have been much greater; therefore conception would have been quicker and easier, with multiple births far more frequent than they are now, when even "those who are most fertile give birth at most to one child in a single year." In the state of innocence man would have remained a vegetarian and would therefore have avoided the obesity that has begun to beset him since he became a carnivore. Since nothing in the state of integrity could have been unpleasant, he would likewise have retained a pleasant odor; man must have smelled "delicate and delightful" before he fell into sin. His power of vision then must have exceeded that of the eagle now, and his physical strength must have enabled him to handle lions and bears as we handle puppies nowadays. "Man would never have experienced the inconveniences of old age; his forehead would never have developed wrinkles; and his feet, his hands, and any other part of his body would not have become weaker or more inactive."[12]

The intellectual powers of man must have been equally magnificent. Regardless of how many generations of men might have followed Adam, it would have been unnecessary to instruct them about the mystery of human origins. Not merely the transmission of this information through the sinless generations of immortal men, but the intuition by which Adam recognized Eve as bone of his bone and flesh of his flesh would have taught the descendants of Adam about their beginnings in the creating action of God.[13] In the *Lectures on Genesis* Luther—or one of his editors—was willing to say that if it had not been for the fall, Adam and his descendants would never have needed civil government but would have lived in social peace and domestic tranquillity automatically. (Elsewhere in his writings, however, Luther indicated that even apart from sin government was necessary as a means of ordering human life, as there was a government in heaven among the holy angels, who neither have sinned nor can sin.)[14] Adam's intellectual powers before the fall entitled him to the name "philosopher." From the statement of the book of Genesis that Adam gave names to all the animals, Luther concluded that he must have been endowed with a remarkable insight into the true nature and inner disposition of the other creatures. He understood the trees and herbs, and he even had "the most dependable knowledge of the stars and of the whole of astronomy."[15]

Even more remarkable than the physical and intellectual endowments of primitive man were his moral gifts. Luther was especially impressed with the meaning of sex in the state of innocence. He tried to imagine sexual desire without lust. He spoke of "a transcendent decency, not shame and embarrassment" in sexual intercourse under the conditions of primitive innocence. Adam felt an "overwhelmingly passionate love," which was a "need for a delightful and full relationship or cohabitation in both love and holiness." Repeatedly Luther emphasized that in the state of integrity sexual union would have been an expression not of libido but of obedience toward God. Like Augustine, he interpreted the involuntary nature of sexual desire as a symptom of the sin that corrupts all of life. But Luther found it possible, in at least one place, to say that sexual union would have been "most delightful" in the state of innocence because it would have been unaccompanied by shame and sin. Indeed, "after the proclamation of the name of God it [procreation] is the most important activity Adam and Eve in the state of innocence could carry on—as free from sin in doing this as they were in praising God." The symbol for this uninhibited and holy innocence was the nakedness of Adam and Eve before the fall.[16]

The Problem of the Fall

Nevertheless this very effort to interpret the state of innocence as a historical reality involved Luther in the danger of making Adam and Eve so pure and noble that the historicity of the fall was difficult to maintain. How could so superior a being have been deceived by the serpent? Everything Luther said to make the fall appear serious also made it appear incredible. Therefore he was obliged eventually to resort to a definition of the *status integritatis* as "the innocence of a child."[17] In the early church Irenaeus described Adam and Eve as children; Paul Tillich has also spoken about "dreaming innocence" as the perennial meaning of the story of Paradise.[18] Reasoning a posteriori from the fall, Luther said: "I call it the innocence of a child because Adam was, so to speak, in a middle position and yet could be deceived by Satan and fall into disaster, as he did." A little later, in the very midst of an encomium of the powers of primitive man, he had to stop to clarify this point again: Adam "was righteous and upright . . . endowed with extraordinary perception and an upright yet imperfect will. For perfection was postponed until the spiritual life after the physical one." So Luther recognized that the term "perfection" has an unavoidably teleological force, as the Greek word *teleiosis* makes clear. Hence he was obliged to posit the thesis that even in the state of innocence this temporal life would have been followed by another and an eternal life.

From this thesis it is clear that Luther's interpretation of the meaning of death in relation to the state of innocence also had to be paradoxical. Throughout Christian history theologians have defined death as "the wages of sin." But they have also found it necessary to define it, in relation to the process of time in which life moves, as simply termination.[19] The first definition has caused them to see mortality as something unnatural, added to the human constitution because of sin but not an original part of man's created temporal existence. The second definition has come from the recognition that the idea of an infinite senescence, even the senescence of an innocent being, is an absurdity. Luther took the occasion of the story of Eve's creation to expound his notion that, after living out his intended time span, Adam would have fallen asleep among the roses—which, as we shall see, were not yet equipped with thorns—and that "during that sleep he would have been changed and transported into the spiritual life without experiencing any pain, just as he did not realize that his body was being opened and that a rib, with flesh, was being taken out."[20] Nothing so aptly illustrates the problems created by a historical exegesis of Genesis as this need to acknowledge the naturalness of death in the midst of a discussion whose primary theme was the gravity of sin and the terror of death as the wages of sin. Dying belongs to time and history, and the only way to eliminate it from the primitive state is to remove the primitive state from time and history; yet both theology and scholarship obliged Luther to immerse the primitive state in history.

A Second Creation

A fundamental transformation of the cosmos by the fall of man was the inevitable corollary of this historical exegesis. "Before sin," according to Luther, "the sun was brighter, the water purer, the trees more fruitful, and the fields more fertile." He became especially extravagant in his description of the serpent before the fall of man. It walked erect, like a rooster or a peacock. It ate fruit rather than earth, and it had neither scales nor a poisonous tail. Thus the serpent was a beautiful and friendly beast, indeed a pet. Other animals had likewise been perverted by man's sin. The very distinction between wild animals and tame animals was a result of sin; for though these animals were all created at the beginning, man's fall into sin had rendered some of them dangerous to him. About other noxious creatures, however, Luther advanced a more startling suggestion. "Darnel, wild oats, weeds, nettles, thorns, thistles . . . poisons, injurious vermin. . . . all these were brought in through sin." Toads, flies, butterflies, caterpillars, bedbugs, and the like were all the result of the fall. And if there had been no fall, there would have been perpetual spring, without snow or frost. In such a climate man would not have needed houses but could have gone on living in the garden.[21]

Contrary to his own intention Luther was thus compelled to posit a second creation as a consequence of the fall. Entire orders of creatures came into being not "in the beginning" but after the disobedience of Adam and Eve. One theological reason for reading the story of the creation and the story of the fall as history has been to distinguish between created existence and sin and thus to avoid the implication that time is inherently evil.[22] If the two stories of creation and the fall are not read as historical accounts, they may easily be combined into one story, whose meaning is the sinfulness of any life within time. On the other hand, if the two stories are read as historical accounts, the disharmony between man and his environment becomes one outcome of human sin. Not merely man's attitude toward God nor his treatment of his fellow men nor his association with his fellow creatures, but the entire structure of creation and the cosmos has been altered. Earthquakes and snow, toads and lice all owe their origin not to the love of God but to his wrath. In fact, all of temporal existence as it is now constituted owes its origin to the wrath of God. From this it is only one step of logic to the conclusion that any life within time would have been sinful—the very conclusion that the historical exegesis of the stories of creation and fall was intended to obviate!

The irony of that logic is matched by the irony that appears in the notion of a fallen creation. At its most profound, this notion symbolizes the intuition that the harmony of life with life is the will of the Creator and that man and his fellow creatures are involved together in the whole web of existence. Luther's historical exegesis of Genesis, with its vivid if slightly bizarre colors, could be an effective antidote to exploitation. But this same exegetical method led him to take literally the command of Genesis: "And have dominion." The dominion apparently applied even to the curse that followed sin. "Inasmuch as [the earth] sustained the sinning human being, it is also compelled, like a tool, to bear the curse. . . . The Holy Spirit . . . distinguishes between the earth and Adam: the curse he turns aside to the earth, but the person he preserves." Believing as he did that Adam was a vegetarian, Luther suggested that in the state of perfection the human race "would have made use of the creatures only for the admiration of God and for a holy joy which is unknown to us in this corrupt state of nature."[23]

The Technical Autonomy of Science

Quite unexpectedly, however, the historical exegesis of the Genesis accounts by the Reformers did open the way for a reconsideration of all these conclusions. If one is to make sense of these accounts as an accurate record of what the universe is like and of how it came to be, one must turn to other sources to supplement the scanty information in the Bible. Despite his well-publicized remark about "that fool" Copernicus, who was trying to "turn all of astronomy upside down," Luther insisted that the study of the natural world, like the study of law or politics, had a technical autonomy and was to be permitted to carry out its research according to its own canons. Rejecting an allegory of Augustine, he declared that "the astronomers are the experts from whom it is most convenient to get what may be discussed about these subjects." "No science," he argued, "should stand in the way of another science, but each should continue to have its own mode of procedure and its own terms."[24]

This application to the relation between science and theology of Luther's doctrine of the two realms is of fundamental importance for any effort to redefine the task of the Christian intellectual in the context of Reformation thought. It meant that the basic concern of theology with the doctrine of creation was not with the matter of origins but with the meaning of mystery, and that the task of biblical exegesis was to probe that meaning in the text of Scripture. The career of Luther as a professor makes clear that Luther's solution for "the conflict of the faculties" was just such a recognition of the division of labor among various disciplines.[25] In this recognition he provided a basis for the Christian intellectual to carry out his thought and research in freedom from the domination of theology but not in indifference to its message. The "history of the warfare of science with theology in Christendom"[26] has issued in both freedom and indifference, at least until the recovery by modern thought of many of the fundamental insights of Reformation thought. Both science and theology have begun to discover that mutual indifference is no solution to the problem of their warfare, and it is significant that in the thought of such Christian intellectuals as Karl Heim and C. F. von Weizsäcker the thought of the Reformation has once more received serious attention.[27]

IV
The Doctrine of Creation

When the confessions of Luther's Reformation—some of them written by Luther himself, others by his disciples—took up the task of defending and summarizing his theology, the doctrine of creation was inevitably one of the issues to which they turned. Not Luther's quasi-historical speculations about the primitive state of man before the fall but the full range of the doctrine was their concern. In this chapter we shall summarize the doctrine of creation in these confessions, and in chapter five we shall seek to develop some of their thought more fully. In chapter six, with which Part Two of this volume begins, we shall deal with the doctrine of man in these confessions, as an introduction to our consideration of "Christian thought and the humanities."

Seeking as they did to declare the orthodox Christian faith on the basis of the Scriptures, the confessions of Luther's Reformation articulated their doctrine of man within the fundamental biblical category of "creature." But because this is often more implicit than explicit in their theological discussions, an exposition of the doctrine of creation in the confessions cannot content itself with merely reciting their outright statements on the doctrine of creation; these are sparse and disappointingly brief.[1] It must also probe into the way their anthropology and Christology, as well as their polemics, proceeded within the confines of the doctrine of creation. They could say as little as they did about it even in the doctrine of man at least partly because every theological statement about man was predicated of the subject: man the creature. For an understanding of their doctrine of man, consequently, the doctrine of creation and of God the Creator is central.[2]

The Medieval Background

In medieval Thomism the doctrine of creation provided a measure of sanction for the importation of Aristotelian metaphysics into Christian theology. Both Scripture and the *Physica,* so it was thought, had spoken about the world; both Scripture and the *De anima* had discussed the human soul. If, as Thomas maintained, the existence of God could be demonstrated from the creation to anyone familiar with the creation,[3] then it necessarily followed that an understanding of creation—though not, as we have seen, of *creatio ex nihilo*—was also accessible to the unaided human mind.[4] To this quantum of knowledge there had to be added the revealed doctrine that the author of this creation was alone eternal and underived. Revelation also disclosed that he was at the same time Father, Son, and Holy Spirit, trine in person and single in essence.[5] But short of this, reason could come to know the creation. Combined as it was with the doctrine of the analogy of being,[6] this entire assumption made possible the synthesis in Thomism between the biblical doctrine of creation and Aristotelian ontology, with all the implications and consequences of that synthesis in many areas.

But this entire complex of thought was by no means the exclusive property of Thomism. Large segments of Reformation theology proceeded in a remarkably similar manner. Underlying this situation is an ambiguity evident in the theology of the Reformers, an ambivalence in their attitude toward the medieval doctrines of God and Christ. The Reformers claimed to share the doctrines of God and of Christ that were the common property of all Christendom. This claim made itself known in their acceptance of the ancient, so-called "ecumenical" creeds. In keeping with this claim Article I of the Augsburg Confession was able to refer to God as *essentia,* despite all the metaphysical connotations which that word had acquired since its original incorporation into the Latin doctrine of the Trinity.[7]

As a matter of fact, however, the difference between Rome and Reformation was greater than the largely conventional phraseology of its several articles indicates. How great that difference was in the doctrine of Christ's person became evident in the controversies between Calvinism and Lutheranism. They both claimed adherence to the ancient creeds and to the decrees of the ecumenical councils, including especially the Council of Chalcedon.[8] They both likewise professed to stand in continuity with the medieval church and its supposedly orthodox interpretation of those Christological creeds and decrees. But by the time the full implications of their respective Christologies had been explored in the controversy, it became clear that they diverged not only from each other but from the medieval interpretation as well. Significantly, they continued to maintain their claim of harmony with the Christological consensus of the ancient church.

A divergence also appeared between Rome and the Reformation in the doctrine of God, specifically in the doctrine of God as Creator. Proceeding from his understanding of the nature of faith, Luther had insisted that the doctrine of creation, too, be seen in the light of Christ.[9] That is to say, Luther sought to restore the words "I believe" to their position at the head of the creed. Before saying, "God the Father Almighty, Creator of heaven and earth," the creed declared: "I believe." But the faith of the Christian believer was derived from the forgiving and reconciling act of God the Father in

Christ as communicated by the Holy Spirit. It was no mere *Fürwahrhalten* (holding to be true) according to the confessions, as Ritschl maintained,[10] but it was always trust in the God who was described by the doctrine of the Trinity. And so Luther could speak as though the choice lay between Christ and atheism, with no third possibility.[11] This was true not only of redemption but also of creation. For the theology of the Reformation confessions, therefore, creation was a Trinitarian doctrine in its very nature and central structure.

When Reformation theology has failed to take this insight seriously, it has dealt with the creed as though the first article could be considered apart from the second. In much of the nineteenth century it slighted creation for the sake of redemption, as Lütgert has pointed out.[12] But Max Lackmann has shown the extent of the continuity between the classic Protestant treatments of creation and their Latin predecessors.[13] The ontological discussions of such Protestant theologians consequently took on many of the characteristics of Thomistic ontology. Some Protestant theologians even advanced a form of the theory of the analogy of being.[14] These were in many cases the same theologians whose expositions of the authority of the Scriptures were the most exhaustive in theological history. If anything, the Reformation versions of this entire problem have been complicated by the fact that the Protestant churches had no official metaphysics.

"In the Context of All Creatures"

As a theology that sought to be loyal to revelation, the theology of the confessions attempted not to read into the biblical view an interpretation of reality that was not there nor to resolve tensions which the biblical view left unresolved; here as elsewhere it taught that "harmonization" of biblical paradoxes was unwarranted.[15]

In addressing themselves to the problem of being, and particularly to the problem of human existence, therefore, the confessions did not engage in the quest of logic and philosophy for the differentia between the being of man and the being of other creatures; man was created "in the context of all creatures."[16] Such a quest would appear to be somewhat suspect from the viewpoint of the New Testament, at least until one has defined what it means to be a creature in the first place.[17] How suspect such a quest would be is apparent from the New Testament's use of "man." There seem to be only two places (Matt. 12 : 12; I Cor. 15 : 39) in which the word "man" is definitely used to contrast man and the other creatures; and one of these, I Corinthians 15 : 39, certainly does more to accentuate the problem of man's distinctiveness than to solve it.

The declaration that man is created "in the context of all creatures" would receive substantiation from the fact that in the New Testament a dominant element in the use of the term "man" was the contrast between man and God, creature and Creator, rather than the contrast between man the creature and other creatures. Man may be false, just as long as God is true (Rom. 3 : 4). Even a man doing divine things remains a man and does not become a god (Acts 10 : 26). If a man permits some apparently divine feature to delude him into believing that he is a god and not a man, he becomes guilty of idolatry by not giving God the glory, and he is punished (Acts 12 : 22, 23.) To refuse to see Jesus Christ as the Suffering Servant is to think humanly, not divinely (Matt. 16 : 23). Indeed, it is not merely the wisdom of God which is greater than the wisdom of men; but the foolishness of God is wiser than the wisdom of men, his weakness stronger than their strength (I Cor. 1 : 23.) For the confessions, as for the New Testament, this was the basic contrast.

This qualitative difference between God and man would seem to mean that for the confessions man could not be known apart from the God who created him. The confessions stated this explicitly with regard to the depths of human sin; they seem to imply it with regard to the full meaning of his creation by God. The very fact of the *imago Dei* meant that man must be understood *coram Deo.*[18] For the confessions, then, the best study of mankind was not man but the word of God. For "by the word of the Lord were the heavens made." Hence the central element in this doctrine of creation is the insistence upon the primacy of the divine initiative in the creative act. It is from this insistence that the *creatio ex nihilo* proceeds, and not vice versa. Thus, as chapter two has noted, both the Hebrew and the Greek terms for "create" in the Bible are used in three ways: (1) for the creation recorded in Genesis; (2) for the creation that goes on even today, what dogmaticians call *creatio continua;* (3) for an eschatologically interpreted "new creation." Common to all three is the primacy of the divine initiative.

All three concepts of creation converge in such passages as Isaiah 45 and Psalm 139. These chapters therefore help form the exegetical basis of the confessions' contention that even after the fall, man continues to be "God's creature and handiwork."[19] Creation cannot mean only *creatio ex nihilo* for the confessions, for it is in interpreting the idea of creation that some of their most existential statements are made. Perhaps the most striking such statement is Luther's masterful summary of the primitive meaning of creation by the initiative of God, even though he may use other materials and instruments: "Creatures are only the hands, channels, and means through which God bestows all blessings. For example, he gives to the mother breasts and milk for her infant, and he gives grain and all kinds of fruits from the earth for man's nourishment—things which no creature could produce by himself."[20]

A Christocentric Doctrine

The basic meaning of creation in the Reformation confessions, then, was the priority and initiative of the divine action. But for Luther no divine action was separable from the divine action in Jesus Christ, though distinctions might be made for the sake of convenience. Nor could there be any true faith apart from him, not even true faith in the Creator. Therefore the doctrine of creation in the confessions cannot be relegated to some sort of natural theology, as though everyone understood the first article and only Christians understood the second article. The confessions concerned themselves with the doctrine of creation because it was a Christian doctrine and a Christocentric one. Christ revealed the creation because he was at once Creator and creature. He was thus the revelation of the Creator to the creature, but he was also the revelation of the creature to itself. The Christ of redemption also made clear the meaning of creation.

This had been adumbrated already in the Old Testament. It was specifically the God of the covenant who in his name made clear what it means "to be."[21] Against a metaphysical dualism like that of Marcion, which would separate the Lord of creation from the Lord of salvation, the Old Testament treated the God of the covenant as the Creator; this is the theological significance of the second creation account (Gen. 2 : 4 ff.). The close relation between creation and salvation appears also in the story of the flood. There the rainbow was instituted as a sign of God's convenant for the protection of the people involved in that covenant from the ravages of the created universe (Gen. 8 : 21, 22; 9 : 12–17). It is apparently an exegesis of this story when the Apology of the Augsburg Confession asserts that "we are necessarily subjected to the laws of the seasons and to the change of winter and summer as ordinances of God."[22] In a similar tone it speaks elsewhere of "this universe and the fixed movement of the stars" as "truly ordinances of God . . . preserved by God."[23]

The New Testament likewise posited a continuity between the creation and the new creation. The God who caused the light to shine out of darkness was the same God who, through Jesus Christ, shone in men's hearts (II Cor. 4 : 6). The original creative fiat, "Let there be light," was, so to say, reinforced when the Creator gave the light that enlightened every man coming into the world (John 1 : 9). And so, as Schweizer has demonstrated, when the Gospel of John has Jesus state, "I am the light," this identifies his coming and his being with the creative action of God.[24] The origin of the aeons was in the speaking of God (Heb. 11 : 3), but the God who spoke in the creation and continued to speak in the prophets had spoken finally in his Son, through whom he also made those aeons (Heb. 1 : 2).

It was, therefore, in harmony with the New Testament and the orthodox tradition when the confessions spoke of Christ as "this truthful and almighty Lord, our Creator and Redeemer Jesus Christ."[25] Interestingly, the New Testament descriptions of Christ's participation in the creation are not made so directly. It usually relates Christ to the act of creation by means of a preposition, suggesting that neither the creation nor the new creation can be understood in its own light, nor, strictly speaking, in the light of the other; but that both must be understood in the light of the God who is the Father of Christ.

The indirect form of ascribing creation to Christ also served as a reminder of the other New Testament statements that interpreted Christ as creature. This was the sense of the polemic of the Formula of Concord against the theory "that Christ did not assume his flesh and blood from the virgin Mary but brought it along from heaven,"[26] in other words, that Christ was not a creature as other men are. In opposition to this the Formula defends the thesis "that according to the flesh or according to his assumed human nature Christ is a creature."[27] As the essence of man was his creatureliness, so Christ's humanity "is in its essence and all its essential attributes—sin alone excepted—identical with ours."[28]

The creatureliness of Christ was the theme of such New Testament passages as Romans 8 : 3, which had figured in the controversies surrounding the Formula of Concord.[29] Particularly interesting in this connection are those passages which apply the title "man" to Jesus. When the devil demanded that he demonstrate his divine Sonship, Jesus replied not by pointing to power but by citing God's demands upon him and upon all men (Luke 4 : 4). The Sabbath was made for man and not man for the Sabbath, just as the Son of Man was Lord also of the Sabbath (Mark 2 : 27, 28). Without entering into all the problematics of the question, one can certainly see an indication of this same emphasis in the Adam-Christ schematization of Romans 5 and I Corinthians 15, a schematization which the confessions used to demonstrate the necessity of Christ's true humanity for his true obedience.[30] What was glorified in Christ, according to the confessions, was his humanity.[31]

Although the chief concentration of Reformation theology was always the relation between God and man rather than the relation between God and the universe, the confessions of Luther's Reformation were nevertheless compelled to clarify their doctrine of creation in order to define their doctrine of man. In chapter six we shall turn to their doctrine of man in more detail, but in the present context their doctrine of creation shows some of the lines of development that could proceed from Luther's teaching, as described in chapter three. For here the "biblical realism" of Luther's language transcends the limitations of his sometimes bizarre attempts at historical exegesis, to produce a doctrine of creation that can interpret natural philosophy sympathetically while still retaining its theological identity. In chapter five we shall seek to develop the implications of this doctrine of creation a little further, drawing upon Psalm 139, which, as we have seen, is one of the biblical sources of the confessional doctrine.

V
The Mystery of the Known

"Mystery" is often little more than another word for ignorance. A mystery story is one in which the detective identifies the culprit, "solving the mystery." Again, the source of the Nile was a mystery to antiquity. Mystery is in inverse ratio to knowledge. Hence the increase of knowlege about "natural philosophy" in modern times has managed to exorcise much of the mystery surrounding man and his world in the age of the Reformation. And as the area of the knowable increases still more, Christian thought may expect the term "mystery" to decline yet further in significance and value.

This view of mystery as the quantity of the Unknown appears in such statements of Luther as the warning that "it is no disgrace, even if we lack knowledge about some mysteries of the Holy Scriptures. The apostles had their own individual revelations, about which it is presumptuous and foolish to engage in extensive discussions."[1] But later in the same commentary he was able to declare that the patriarchs of the Old Testament "understood the mystery of the Trinity, which is preached to us in clear and plain language."[2] On the one hand, mystery is a matter of private revelation, into which it is foolish to pry; it is the quantity of the Unknown. But on the other hand, even the mystery of the Trinity can be "understood" and by the patriarchs at that, and it can be articulated in clear and plain language; it is a quality of the Known. The former conception of mystery as the quantity of the Unknown has predominated in the history of theology, as chapter two has indicated; but it has never satisfied the deepest insights of Christian reverence, which has repeatedly gone on to recognize the mysterious quality of the Known. In chapter one we have analyzed one of the most exciting and influential attempts in modern Christian thought to formulate a redefinition of mystery and have raised some questions about its adequacy. In the present chapter we shall conclude Part One of this volume by attempting a brief statement of the meaning of mystery, based upon Psalm 139. For although Luther did not compose a separate commentary on this Psalm, it did provide him with the key to the understanding of other passages of the Bible.[3] And, as we have seen in chapter four, it also provided the Reformation confessions with biblical support for the idea of "continuous creation," in spite of sin.

Psalm 139

1. O Lord, thou hast searched me and known me!
2. Thou knowest when I sit down and when I rise up; thou discernest my thoughts from afar.
3. Thou searchest out my path and my lying down, and art acquainted with all my ways.
4. Even before a word is on my tongue, lo, O Lord, thou knowest it altogether.
5. Thou dost beset me behind and before, and layest thy hand upon me.
6. Such knowledge is too wonderful for me; it is high, I cannot attain it.
7. Whither shall I go from thy Spirit? Or whither shall I flee from thy presence?
8. If I ascend to heaven, thou art there! If I make my bed in Sheol, thou art there!
9. If I take the wings of the morning and dwell in the uttermost parts of the sea,

10. even there thy hand shall lead me, and thy right hand shall hold me.

11. If I say, "Let only darkness cover me, and the light about me be night,"

12. even the darkness is not dark to thee, the night is bright as the day; for darkness is as light with thee.

13. For thou didst form my inward parts, thou didst knit me together in my mother's womb.

14. I praise thee, for thou art fearful and wonderful. Wonderful are thy works! Thou knowest me right well;

15. my frame was not hidden from thee, when I was being made in secret, intricately wrought in the depths of the earth.

16. Thy eyes beheld my unformed substance; in thy book were written, every one of them, the days that were formed for me, when as yet there was none of them.

17. How precious to me are thy thoughts, O God! How vast is the sum of them!

18. If I would count them, they are more than the sand. When I awake, I am still with thee.

In its review of the mysterious knowledge that is too wonderful for human attainment (v. 6), the Psalm sounds five closely related themes that have echoed throughout religious history. These motifs recur so often that we are probably justified in looking upon them as paradigmatic. For their ultimate source we should probably have to look into the earliest history of man. In the history of religion each of these motifs has helped to define mystery as the quantity of the Unknown and hence has enabled the priests, who were endowed with special entree to the supernatural, to open up the secrets of life, both divine and human.

The Quantity of the Unknown

The primordial representative of the Unknown is the darkness. When the Psalmist considers flight into darkness as a journey into the Unknown (vv. 11–12), he means that those who are threatened by the mystery of the Unknown are "in darkness" even when there is light; for "there is nothing but darkness for the world, since such a light never rises for it in its adversity."[4] Or, as Luther says elsewhere, "in Scriptural language, 'to see [God's] face' means to recognize him correctly";[5] such visual imagery about the mystery of the Unknown is further evidence that the terror of the darkness is somewhere near the center of man's attitude toward mystery. Both in his view of history and in his doctrine of the atonement Luther gave voice to a "dramatic dualism."[6] This was so sharp as to call forth accusations of Manichaeism.[7] But in fact he was echoing earlier Christian language, especially that of some Greek fathers.[8] He was also articulating the fundamental intuition that there are two forces contending over life, not merely one, and that of these two forces the unknown dark is the *mysterium tremendum et fascinans.*[9] "Burning bright in the forests of the night" shines the mystery of the Unknown.

A second motif is the power of the past. The religion of the tribe is often the history of the tribe, the story of the eponymous ancestor in whose life wondrous events took place and, before that, the account of the process (now duplicated and reenacted in ritual) by which the gods once created the world.[10] Access to this past and to its mystery is through remembrance and worship. The liturgical formula of the Psalm (v. 14) "Wonderful are thy works!" refers, in the setting of Israel's faith, to the deeds of God in the history of the people—the exodus, the crossing of the Red Sea, and behind this the creation of the world in six days.[11] As Luther noted, the prophets "exalt this history of the exodus from Egypt as the high point of all the other histories, making frequent mention of it, developing it in detail, and arranging other histories on the basis of it."[12] Enshrined as it is in the remembrance and ritual, the past is not directly available or immediately known. As "past," it is an Unknown; as the mysterious Unknown to which one looks for an explanation of our origins, the past has a religious claim upon one. From this claim is derived the authority of the Scriptures where the past is recited, as well as the sacredness of the process of tradition by which the unknown past is continually being brought into the present.[13]

Sometimes it is unknown places rather than unknown times that have the charm of mystery about them. The Psalmist speaks about taking the wings of the morning and dwelling in the uttermost parts of the sea (v. 9). As George H. Williams has shown, the role of the "Land of Promise" in Jewish history or of the "Holy Land" in Christian history proves something more fundamental than the cliché that distance lends enchantment.[14] It belongs to the religious nature of man to endow with attributes of mystery the inhabitants, the customs, and even the costumes of the undiscovered country. Although "outlandish" and "exotic" have the same denotation, the difference in their connotations—as applied, for example, to costumes—sets "exotic" apart as a term for the mystery of the unknown realms beyond the sea. The Joshua who had first penetrated into the undiscovered country finally became the leader of the people of God. At close range, of course, this mystery disappears; but there is always the lure of the Unknown on the mysterious frontier beyond the horizon.

More mysterious than any undiscovered country is the universe beyond them all. This must be the abode of the Divine; our Father must be in heaven. Hence Psalm 139 speaks of ascending to heaven and of making one's bed in Sheol, the abode of the dead (v. 8). Astral influence and the divinity of planets constituted major tenets of several religious and theological systems surrounding the beginnings of Christianity. "The sky hung low in the first century," as the epigram of Shirley Jackson Case has put it.[15] Therefore those who knew about the stars knew about the gods, but for those without access to such arcane knowledge both the stars and the gods remained shrouded in mystery. The exegesis described in chapter three illustrates how the incidental references to the cosmos in the Bible could be thought to contain and convey the only reliable information about the unknown region of the stars—especially when these references were interpreted in support of various cosmologies that had originally been formulated without the benefit of Christian revelation. Theology denounced science for prying into the mystery of the unknown cosmos and attempting to extract from it secrets that were known but to God. This seemed to imply that if man could learn these secrets, God would have to become less mysterious, that is, less God.

Even when ancient times or dark and distant places have been explored, one great Unknown remains, inscrutable as ever: the mystery of the future. Behind the discussion in Luther's *Bondage of the Will* about whether God can know future contingents is the idea that the mystery of divine Being must be closely related to the unknowability of the future.[16] The Psalmist expresses his amazement that God could know what a man is going to say even before the man does (v. 4) and that God could see a man full-formed before there was even an embryo (v. 16). Soothsayers lay claim to information about the future and thus to possession of a divine mystery. Apologists for certain theological systems have had recourse to this argument when all other proofs failed: at least men could not know the future, and therefore there was still a great Unknown, still a mystery, still a God. Even when these apologists could no longer condemn the acquisition of scientific knowledge as the invasion of God's privileged sanctuary, they could still identify mystery as the quantity of the Unknown about the future.

When mystery is defined in this way as the quantity of the Unknown, Christian thought becomes the enemy of natural philosophy, and the heirs of Luther's Reformation have put themselves into the position of reserving as unknowable the very areas of reality into which natural philosophy was penetrating. The last-ditch stand of such an apologetic has been to push the mysterious still further back into the ancient past or even farther out into the universe, until it has neither cognitive meaning nor religious and ethical relevance. The acceleration of scientific discovery in the past century—which Robert Frost once likened to a hundred-yard dash followed by a pole vault—has made the problem of redefining mystery especially acute. But it is often forgotten that the biblical writers found such redefinition necessary for religious reasons even when their cosmology did not require it. Psalm 139 illustrates this redefinition as well.

The Quality of the Known

When the terror of the darkness has been dispelled by the light, ignorance gives way to knowledge and hidden reality becomes visible. But as the Psalmist discovers that he cannot successfully hide in the dark, so he finds that mystery does not vanish with the coming of the light (v. 12). On the contrary, the blessing of vision, the gift of the vision of God, serves to deepen rather than to dispel the mystery.[17] The inaugural vision granted to Isaiah provoked his exclamation of awe: "Woe is me! For I am lost . . . for my eyes have seen the king, the Lord of hosts!" (Is. 6 : 5). The vision of the divine power present in Christ and evident in the draught of fishes evoked from Peter a similar prayer: "Depart from me, for I am a sinful man, O Lord" (Luke 5 : 8). Not the darkness but the vision of the Son of Man stirred the reverence of the seer of the Apocalypse: "When I saw him, I fell at his feet as though dead" (Rev. 1 : 17). In both the Old and the New Testament man's vision of God is not merely the effort to fill in the gaps of ignorance between the bits of his knowledge, but it is also the attempt to come to terms with all the dimensions of his knowledge. It brings him face to face not with one being among beings, not even with a Supreme Being, but with the Lord of Being. The New Testament does not specify the meaning of *mysterion* very often, but one of the realities to which it applies this term illustrates this meaning trenchantly. The Epistle to the Ephesians refers to the relation between a man and a woman as "a great mystery." Certainly this is a mystery to an adolescent, part of the quantity of the Unknown. But greater maturity does not dissipate this mystery. Sexual "knowledge" in the Hebraic sense includes the experience of even greater mystery as a quality of the Known.[18] So the vision of God in the history of his people and in the life, death, and resurrection of his Son makes the mystery of life and being even more haunting, and it inspires an awe that is more reverent than ignorance and deeper than doubt.

Similarly, although the grandeur of Christian antiquity may stir feelings of worship, it may also reinforce the decision to let bygones be bygones. It can stir feelings of worship if the worshiper manages to identify himself with the past of the church, effecting a congruence between that past and his past. Sheer antiquity, without such an identification, may fascinate with the mystery of the long ago and far away; but American schoolboys were not the first to use "ancient history" as a synonym for "musty and irrelevant." Only when the ancient history can be seen as *my* history does it spring to life, becoming a new and more fascinating mystery because of my involvement in it. As Luther said: "It is all the word of God, true. But word of God or not, I must know and take note who it is to whom the word of God is addressed."[19] Right after the doxology, "Wonderful are thy works" (v. 14), the Psalmist goes on to describe the wonderful work involved in the origin of his own existence (vv. 14–16). The creative power at work in the past of the world, the redemptive power evident in the past of Israel—all of this mysterious power the Psalmist possesses existentially: "Thou didst knit me together in my mother's womb" (v. 13). When ancient history becomes autobiography in the setting of the liturgy, the past lays hold upon the believer and he owns the mystery: *Credo in unum Deum*. One implication of this confession in the Creed, as Luther's catechisms illustrate, is the affirmation that what is sovereign over the past is likewise sovereign over my past.[20]

Within this past the religion of Israel looked back at Abraham the nomad as the father of the faithful and at the exodus from Egypt as the disclosure of its destiny. Therefore it could not equate mystery with the exotic allure of the undiscovered country. For after the country had been discovered, after Jericho had fallen and Israel had conquered cities it had not built, there came further and deeper revelations of universal love. This love was not subject to either manipulation or transportation; the ark of the covenant did not exhaust its power, and Israel did not lead the Lord God across the Jordan. The call to love for the Creator and love for the creature was as universal as creation itself. For his *chesed,* "steadfast love,"[21] was evident to the eyes of faith everywhere, penetrating all the countries, whether discovered or undiscovered: "even there thy hand shall lead me, and thy right hand shall hold me" (v. 10). Also in the unknown land beyond the uttermost parts of the sea the known trustworthiness of this *chesed* had been woven into an invisible net that gave support and rescue and meaning to life. The praise of the steadfast love of God in its universal power reached its zenith in the fifty-third chapter of Isaiah, on which Luther prepared a number of expositions, which were collected into a full-length commentary in 1544.[22] As Luther's own example demonstrates, the more a believer comes to know about this steadfast love, the more subtle its mystery grows.

Thus the reliability of the love of God remained unshaken even by the vast enigma of the cosmos. "If I ascend to heaven, thou art there! If I make my bed in Sheol, thou art there!" (v. 8). In this prayer the Thou being addressed is affirmed to be the Lord both of the cosmos and of the covenant. As chapter two has suggested, the faith of Israel did not base its understanding of the covenant with God upon the reliability of the cosmos, but elevated the nature festivals into celebrations of the history of the covenant. The assurance that the universe was friendly was an extrapolation from the reliability of Yahweh as the Thou of the covenant. For Christian *spiritualité* Psalm 91 and the story of the Flood summarized this conviction that no cosmic threat could ultimately destroy the foundation of faith. The threats known to the biblical writers were those of which Psalm 91 speaks. Their universe was compact, if not very tidy. They did not know the galaxies that lay beyond the ceiling of the tent, but what excited their awe was the revelation that human life could have a purpose whatever the size and nature of the cosmos. For the God of the biblical writers transcended all world views, including the world views of the biblical writers. The mystery, then, is not simply the quantity of the vast Unknown in the cosmos, but the quality of the Known, affirmed by the faith and the hope which expect to "see the heaven, moon, and stars correctly, not as we see them now in this world."[23]

As revelation does not provide data about the structure of the cosmos, so it also leaves the lineaments of the future inscrutable. Luther repeatedly pointed out that "all the prophets . . . teach and rebuke the people of their time, and they proclaim the coming and the kingdom of Christ," acting both as as "forth-speakers" and as "fore-seers."[24] Yet it would be a mistake to conclude that faith looks upon the future as mysterious merely because it is inscrutable. Even more overwhelming than the realization of God's knowledge about the future is the conviction of God's care in the future (vv. 17–18). The Psalmist does not know what will happen next, and his God will not tell him. But his God will not be dethroned, whatever may happen next. If we lose, we still cannot lose. The deepest meaning of the divine mystery is not insight into the future but openness toward the future. An alternate translation of verse 18 would be: "Were I to come to the end, I would still be with thee."[25] The future now becomes one dimension of the mystery disclosed in the past and operative in the present. To acknowledge that mystery means to open oneself to the unknown future, with all its threats and all its possibilities, and to do so in dedication, commitment, and trust. The history of Christian devotion is full of such expressions of surprise, as men found themselves facing the future more courageously than they ever thought was possible for mere mortals; in fact, both Cyprian and Athanasius argued for the resurrection on this basis.[26] Even the prospect of one's own dissolution takes on a new appearance when the Unknown, who had become the Enemy, now becomes the Friend.

Such a restatement of the biblical view of creation as mystery is made necessary by the fuller implication of the Bible itself. In turn, it also makes possible the reopening of communication between Christian thought and natural philosophy. For it asks Christian thought to speak as a faithful interpreter of the charge laid upon it, without giving it an assignment it cannot carry; and it asks science to speak from within the canons of its own discipline. In this way, as the concluding discussion of chapter three has suggested, such a redefinition of mystery may also be a restatement of basic Reformation teachings.

Part Two

Christian Thought and the Humanities

VI
The Doctrine of Man

Although the theology of Luther's Reformation does provide some ingredients for a re-examination of the relation between Christian thought and natural philosophy, most of the Christian intellectuals associated with the Reformation were specialists in the humanities. The essays gathered in Part Two of this book all deal with the implications of Reformation theology for an understanding of the bearing of Christian thought on the humanistic disciplines. We begin, naturally enough, with the doctrine of man and, as in chapter four, with the summary articulation of that doctrine in the confessions of Luther's Reformation. The confessions themselves yield a useful division for a presentation of the doctrine of man. In attempting to clarify its anthropology, the Formula of Concord distinguished four conditions of man:[1] his state before the fall; his relation to God after the fall; his natural powers after the fall; and his relation to God after conversion.

Man Before the Fall

Because the principal concern of the confessions was with man as he is related to God, the doctrine of man which they presented took its start from the primacy of revelation. And as the depths of human sin since the fall could not be known except by revelation,[2] so it was even less possible for the unaided human mind to conceive of man's condition as it was before the fall. The doctrine of the "primitive state" had to be based upon revelation, as chapter three has shown at some length.

Central to that revelation of God's original plan for man was the doctrine that man is a creature. The origin of human existence did not lie in man's hands, but in God's. And the existence into which man was called by the creative act of God was an existence, as we have seen in chapter four, *sampt allen Kreaturn*.[3] This does not mean merely that God made all creatures, man among them; it means, rather, that man the creation lies in the context of the creation as such, and that man was made to live in affinity with that creation. Thus Luther spoke of man's continuity with the creation in the terror of death, when all creatures joined to tell a man that he must die and when every leaf reminded him of his fate.[4] Similarly, the New Testament described the man in Christ as "a new creation."[5] For man had been created in the company of all creatures, and so he was to be understood.

For the doctrine of the creation to be a relevant as well as a historical statement, however, there must be some relation between the *creatio ex nihilo* and the contemporary world, between the man who was formed of the dust of the earth and the man who is born of human parents today. Without ever developing a speculative interpretation of that relation, the confessions asserted that "I am a creature of God" and again that "God has created me."[6] This assertion, in turn, is the message not of the opening chapters of Genesis but of Psalm 139, as chapter five has sought to show. For that reason, when the Formula of Concord—for reasons which will be mentioned later—wanted to insist that not merely Adam but every man is God's creature, it referred to that Psalm.[7]

But the mere assertion that man is a creature does not exhaust the biblical picture of man. The Bible portrays man as created in the image of God, and the doctrine of the *imago Dei* must always be considered alongside the creatureliness of man.[8] How is that image to be interpreted? Some strains of medieval theology had inclined to the view that the image of God consisted in man's rational capacity.[9] By way of contrast, the Apology of the Augsburg Confession insisted that the phrase "image of God" be interpreted in a religious way rather than in an intellectualistic or moralistic one.[10] The righteousness which God demanded was primarily a righteousness of the first table of the law, a *justitia erga Deum* rather than a mere observance of the prescriptions of the law.[11] And though some of Luther's followers had begun to define the *imago Dei* at least partly in an intellectualistic framework,[12] the confessions, including the Formula of Concord, consistently stressed the religious character of that phrase.[13] This was true even when they quoted church fathers whose doctrine of the *imago Dei* was not altogether free of admixtures of idealism and rationalism.[14] Creation, then, was always creation by God. Original righteousness, the image of God, was also by God and in the sight of God.

The Definition of Sin

Because of the emphasis they put on the religious character of original righteousness and of the image of God, the confessions interpreted sin, too, as a religious rather than principally a moral phenomenon.[15] But in attempting to articulate this they were confronted by the traditional definitions of sin in the medieval church. According to one tradition in medieval theology sin consisted of a "lack of original righteousness" and "concupiscence"; both could be, but did not have to be, interpreted in a moralistic way.[16] As in other areas of theology, so in the definition of sin, the Reformers utilized the definitions that were current in the sixteenth century, but they clarified their meaning. Thus "lack of original righteousness" was interpreted as the inability to come into a proper relation with God,[17] and "concupiscence" became synonymous with egocentricity and rebellion against God.[18] Original righteousness was always righteousness in the sight of God; original sin was always sin in the sight of God. In this sense, at least, Emil Brunner's insistence that the sinner is always a sinner "in the sight of God" is in keeping with the theology of Luther.[19]

But sin was a religious fact for the confessions in a far more vivid sense than the negative statement "lack of the proper relation to God" might indicate. Sin also had its positive side. It was subjection to the wrath of God, and that wrath was real. With Luther, the confessions spoke often about the wrath of God.[20] They refused to rationalize it, as did later Protestants, but saw the wrath of God at work in all the enemies to whom man was now subject as a result of sin.[21] For sin was slavery to the devil.[22] It was death; and as a dead man could not rise of his own accord, so a sinner could not become alive by his own efforts.[23] Over against the attempts to interpret sin as merely a fatal disease which could kill a man if left unchecked, the Formula of Concord emphasized that sin was death itself. There was, of course, good New Testament background for such usage.[24] Sin was bondage, and man was enslaved by sin. Sin was so deep a corruption that only the revelation of God could uncover its ultimate meaning.[25]

And yet even the sinner remained the creature of God. Whatever the confessions asserted concerning the depth of sin and the bondage to the devil must be set in dialectical relation to their continued insistence that God was the Creator also of the sinner. This is the intention underlying the Aristotelian distinction between *substantia* and *accidens* introduced in Article I of the Formula of Concord.[26] Whatever it is that makes a man a man and a creature of God (*substantia*) remains even after the fall. In support of this contention the Formula cited a number of doctrines that would be materially affected by a contrary teaching.[27] Of particular interest in that catalogue was Christology.[28] For if human nature as it was now constituted was a creature of the devil, then the doctrine of Christ faced two alternatives, both of them disastrous: to maintain that Christ's human nature was a creation of the devil; or to maintain that Christ's human nature was not the nature that is common to men.[29] Since either of these alternatives would have destroyed the meaning of the incarnation, the authors of the Formula rejected the thesis that sin had become the *substantia* of man, insisting that in spite of sin man's *substantia,* his creatureliness, remained. Although they were not blind to the possibility that the distinction of *substantia* and *accidens* could lead to the old distinction of *pura naturalia* and *donum superadditum,*[30] they were nevertheless intent upon safeguarding the creatorhood of God and the true human nature of Christ.

Whenever original sin is discussed, one problem inevitably arises: how is original sin transmitted? Augustine had answered the question with a doctrine of seminal transmission, asserting, at least in certain writings, that a man was born sinful because he was the product of the sexual union of a man and a woman.[31] Carrying this point of view even further, Thomas Aquinas had taught that if only Eve had sinned, but not Adam, sin would not have been transmitted to their descendants, since transmitted characteristics were carried only by the father. For this reason Jesus was born sinless in spite of the fact—it will be remembered that Thomas did not teach the immaculate conception of Mary—that he was born of a sinful mother.[32] The confessions devoted relatively little attention to this entire issue. The statement of the Augsburg Confession that all men "who are born according to the course of nature" are sinful, was, as Vilmar points out, "essentially Christological."[33] It did not so much posit an explanation of how sin was transmitted as exclude Christ from the predicate which followed. Following biblical usage, the Formula of

Concord employed the word "seed" in its discussion of original sin,[34] but it did not involve itself in the problematics referred to above. Indeed, the emphasis of the confessions upon the resurrection of the body stood in sharp contrast to any "spiritualism" and, consequently, to any definition of sin as sensuality.

The Problem of Free Will

From what has been said so far about the nature of sin according to the confessions of Luther's Reformation, the suspicion might arise that their doctrine of man was completely deterministic and that they denied man all freedom of choice. There was, as a matter of fact, some ground for such a suspicion. The Renaissance had revived interest in the classical discussions of free will and determinism,[35] and Luther had shown himself willing to use pagan fatalism as supplementary proof for his doctrine of the bondage of the will.[36] Melanchthon, on the other hand, had been deeply concerned with the problem of freedom and natural morality.[37] Because of all this, the confessions found it necessary to distinguish their doctrine of the bondage of the will from mechanistic determinism.

Such a distinction became all the more necessary because of the controversy with Flacius Illyricus. Seeing the gradual growth of natural theology as an opening wedge for a more optimistic interpretation of human capacity, Flacius sought to defend Luther's doctrine of sin by rejecting the natural knowledge of God.[38] By a syllogism strangely parallel to that of Karl Barth,[39] Flacius believed such a rejection to be the only conclusion consistent with Luther's doctrine of man. In opposing Flacius's reasoning, the Formula of Concord taught that man had a certain degree of knowledge about God and the law.[40] But it did not try, as did the later Protestant scholastics, to construct an entire "natural theology," buttressed with all manner of metaphysical proofs for the existence of God.[41] It merely posited some knowledge of God and of the law.

On this latter point, the knowledge of the law, the earlier confessions also had something more to say. Man has the freedom, said the Augsburg Confession, to choose from among the things which reason can grasp.[42] That is to say, man could not choose between those things which were subject to reason and those which were not; but given the area of actions over which reason had control, man could decide which he would accept and which he would reject. As a result those who had applied reason to the solution of human problems had frequently produced admirable answers to ethical problems. Indeed, "Aristotle wrote so well on natural ethics that nothing further needs to be added."[43] For the area of natural ethics was subject to reason, and the Apology explicitly and repeatedly expressed its high praise of civil morals and its deep concern for their preservation, even apart from faith.[44]

In the realm of nature, then, the human will could be said to be free to choose between alternative courses of action. But since faith and the right relation to God could not be subject to reason—for faith was above nature[45]—this freedom to choose had no bearing upon faith. Even though a man's free will *in naturalibus* may lead him to hear the word, this could not be construed as proof that he was free to choose God.[46] On this point Article II of the Formula of Concord was very insistent, even though it was equally insistent in its rejection of Stoic determinism.

Man in the State of Grace

Although the human will was hostile to God and although it could not cooperate with God, yet God made willing persons out of unwilling ones[47] and drew men to him. Our discussion would not be complete without at least a brief presentation of man in the state of grace according to the confessions of Luther's Reformation.

The teaching of the confessions on this point can be summarized in the dictum of Luther: "righteous and a sinner at the same time."[48] Man was "righteous in hope" because, as chapter seven will show at greater length, his "righteousness" was the righteousness of Christ.[49] A great deal of discussion was required in the sixteenth century before this insight was clarified.[50] The controversy which has centered around a crucial passage in the Apology of the Augsburg Confession indicates the scope of that discussion.[51] The relation between justification and sanctification in Melanchthon's theology had gradually been obscured by his definition of faith.[52] In opposition to that definition, Andreas Osiander set an interpretation of justification in which the tension of "righteous and a sinner at the same time" was resolved by reference to a mystic union between Christ and the believer. Because the antithesis between Melanchthon and Osiander presented two alternatives, both of them unacceptable, the Formula of Concord very precisely defined the nature of the "righteousness" in "justification."[53] It ruled out all notions of perfection, for, as the Apology had maintained, the Christian was "righteous in hope" even after baptism.[54] But the Formula also warned that this fact was not to be used as a pretext for an "Epicurean life"[55] or for carnal security.

For while the Christian was "righteous in hope," he was at the same time "a sinner in fact."[56] And the sinner was one who needed repentance and forgiveness. Thus the doctrine of *simul justus et peccator* was not a pretext for carnal security, but quite the opposite. The realization that sin was ever present, even in the saint, and that the righteousness once given in justification must also be actualized in the Christian life was a dynamic for the continued use of the means of grace and for the "exercise" of faith.[57] It was also a stimulant to the Christian hope; for just as the kingdom was still "hidden under the cross,"[58] so also the Christian life had only the first fruits of the Spirit and was based upon an eschatological hope.[59]

As man was created "in the context of all creatures," so, too, he was redeemed in the context of the total creation; for Christ had died for the world, not only for the church.[60] As man's sin was always against God, so, too, he hoped for liberation from sin and death and the devil by the victory of God over these enemies. And as the Christian perceived the incompleteness of his dedication to God, he hoped for deliverance and for the ultimate restoration of his full and authentic humanity.

VII
Divine Justification and Human Justice

Luther's doctrine of justification, some of whose implications for the doctrine of man were summarized in chapter six, ran the constant danger of losing its hold on the doctrine of creation. As the frequent accusation of Manichaeism directed against Luther suggests, this danger threatened to vitiate all the insights into the meaning of creation, discussed in Part One, which Luther and his associates derived from their fresh study of the biblical text. But the charge of Manichaeism involved moral theology as well as doctrinal theology, and an even more frequent accusation against the doctrine of justification in Luther's Reformation is the charge that it cut the moral nerve, especially in the area of social ethics. The line that connected justification to social justice was not easy to draw; the line that separated them was too easy to draw. Ironically, the Latin word *justitia* may sometimes be translated as "justification," sometimes as "justice," and sometimes as "righteousness." The most important and influential of Luther's treatments of *justitia* was his *Lectures on Galatians* of 1535, recently edited and published in the first completely new English translation since the sixteenth century.[1] Its treatment of the analogies between *justitia* as justice and *justitia* as righteousness provides some useful data about Luther's theology in an area that is central for our understanding of the relation between Christian thought and the humanities.

The Demands of Justice

The starting point for Luther's discussion of *justitia* as the gift of righteousness in Christ was his understanding of the nature of the demands laid upon men. Those demands were absolute, and they were addressed to man without any consideration for his ability to meet them or of the peculiar circumstances under which he lived. The law of Moses "is a taskmaster; it demands that we work and that we give. . . . It makes demands on us, and impossible ones at that."[2] The polemical target for much of Luther's *Galatians* was the sort of reasoning that argued from obligation to ability, *a debere ad posse,* concluding either that the law of God could be fulfilled or that it had not been meant as seriously as it sounded. Over against the self-styled defenders of the law who actually mitigated its absolute imperatives in order to make them attainable, Luther insisted on the unconditional character of an unfulfillable law. "The stubborn, proud, and hardhearted, before whose eyes nothing must be set except the law, in order that they may be terrified and humbled" had to be reminded of the absolute character of the demand for *justitia* voiced by the Ten Commandments. Upon them, as upon a beast of burden, "the *justitia* of the law . . . must be placed to oppress" them.[3]

In much of Luther's language about the absolute demand for *justitia* the law was presented as a tyrant. In fact, one of the ways (though not the only way)[4] Luther described the reconciling work of Christ in *Galatians* was the metaphor of a "very joyous duel,"[5] in which Christ overcame the tyranny of sin, death, the devil, and the law by his death and resurrection. "When this duel between the law and Christ was going on . . . Christ . . . having put on our person, serves the law and in supreme innocence suffers all its tyranny."[6] Thus he "has conquered the law in his own person."[7] This duel was made possible by the power of Christ, but it was made necessary by the power of the law and the force of its requirements. Luther recognized that there was a danger in employing such language. He admitted that the apostle's "words sound violently heretical," that "Paul often speaks in a very condescending way about the law" and "chooses . . . loathsome names, which show the power and function of the law clearly and accurately."[8] At the same time, Luther could accuse his opponents of depicting God as "a severe tyrant and a cruel taskmaster, who is not content that I observe and fulfill his law but demands also that beyond the law, which I can easily fulfill, I dress up my obedience with additional qualities and adornments."[9] Their emphasis upon the absoluteness of the command to love God above all things made "God a tyrant and a tormentor who demands of us what we cannot produce."[10] But this argument of Luther's was intended to reject the notion that man could produce the *justitia* of the law by his own natural powers; it was not intended to mitigate in any way the absolute demands of the law.

The refusal to mitigate the demands of *justitia* was important both for *justitia* as righteousness and for *justitia* as justice. Precisely because the law was unrelenting in its demands, it could be "a political restraint upon uncivilized and carnal men to keep them from rushing headlong into all sorts of crimes. The law threatens transgressors with punishment; and if they were not afraid of this, they would do nothing but commit evil. Those who are restrained by the law this way are dominated by the law."[11] Luther recognized that indifference to the absolute claims made upon men by the law could undermine not only the *justitia* announced by the gospel and conferred by grace, but the structures of society as well. Thus the unconcern of those who "do not care at all whether their 'work' . . . is pure or not . . . provides the occasion for all sorts of evil and creates disturbances in both the state and the individual conscience."[12] The demands of *justitia* as justice, like the demands of *justitia* as righteousness, had to be presented without qualification, not because it was possible to achieve an absolute *justitia* in either sense under the conditions of fallen human existence, but because only an unqualified demand could achieve the dual purpose of denouncing sin and thus preparing the way for the gospel and the *justitia* of faith, and of restraining violent crime and thus providing that minimum of external order without which neither church nor state, neither *justitia* as righteousness nor *justitia* as justice, could function.

The Paradox of Justification

As has already been indicated, Luther was well aware that the rigorous insistence on the absoluteness of the demand for *justitia* could not produce complete conformity to that demand. This was true of man outside a state of grace, who could not through the use of his natural powers yield the *justitia* required by God. But Luther insisted that the same was true of man in a state of grace after conversion. His *justitia,* too, remained incomplete and was always held in tension with his continuing *injustitia.* Luther's formula for this tension, which has been discussed at some length in chapter six, was *simul justus et peccator,* "righteous and a sinner at the same time."[13] It meant saying to a person who was in a state of grace: "Brother, it is impossible for you to become so righteous [*justus*] in this life that your body is clear and spotless as the sun. You still have spots and wrinkles, and yet you are holy."[14] Therefore "Christian *justitia* consists in two things: first, in faith, which attributes glory to God; secondly, in God's imputation . . . not for our sakes or for the sake of our worthiness or works but for the sake of Christ himself, in whom we believe."[15] What was lacking in the actual or "formal" *justitia,*[16] was supplied by the forgiveness and imputation of God.

The demands of *justitia* as justice were just as absolute as the demands of *justitia* as righteousness, and just as difficult to reach. In his writings Luther frequently quoted the epigram of Cicero, *summum jus, summa injuria,*[17] in support of the contention that a zeal for absolute *justitia*[18] could lead to the height of injustice. Therefore a prerequisite for the achievement of the kind of *justitia* as justice that was attainable under the conditions of fallen existence was a recognition of the unattainability of the absolute demand for *justitia.* As it was bad theology to ignore this prerequisite for the attainment of *justitia* as righteousness, so it was bad social philosophy to ignore it for the attainment of *justitia* as justice; and Luther claimed that such theology and such social philosophy belonged together. He recognized that "in moral philosophy doing means a good will and right reason to do well." Thus "a lawyer . . . does not suppose that through right reason he will obtain the forgiveness of sins and eternal life." And so "a heathen philosopher is much better than such a self-righteous person, because he remains within his limits, having in mind only honesty and tranquillity, and not mixing divine things with human."[19] By recognizing the limits of his competence and the limited possibilities of *justitia* as justice, the lawyer, whether a Christian or not, showed his superiority to the theologian who believed that *justitia* as righteousness lay within the competence of the natural man.

Therefore some of the axioms erroneously employed by Luther's theological opponents about *justitia* as righteousness were properly applicable to the realm of *justitia* as justice. For example, Luther quoted a little verse, familiar in German and in Latin versions:

> God does not require of any man
> That he do more than he really can,[20]

which his opponents used to prove that "if a man does what lies within him, God infallibly gives him grace."[21] Luther's evaluation of this axiom was: "This is actually a good statement, but in its proper place, that is, in political, domestic, and natural affairs. . . . For this realm has boundaries, and to this realm these statements like 'to do what lies within one' or 'to do as much as I can' properly apply."[22] For radically different reasons it was necessary to acknowledge that both *justitia* as righteousness and *justitia* as justice could be achieved only in limited measure and in a relative sense; but for both senses of *justitia* it was necessary to come to terms with the paradox of absolute demand and relative achievement and to learn to live within the tension and ambiguity created by the paradox.

Resolving the Tension

Both in the realm of *justitia* as righteousness and in the realm of *justitia* as justice, living within the paradox meant refusing to resolve the tension either in the direction of claiming that the absolute demand of *justitia* was within reach or in the direction of settling for the relative achievement of *justitia* as though God did not demand perfect compliance with his will. The first course led to despair, the second to smugness.[23] If *justitia* as righteousness was thought to lie within reach, the inevitable result was despair, for "the heart trembles and continually finds itself loaded down with wagonloads of sins that increase infinitely, so that it deviates further and further from *justitia,* until finally it acquires the habit of despair."[24] On the other hand, it was equally dangerous to scale down the demand for absolute *justitia* to the point where it was equated with respectability; for this produced a presumption of *justitia,* and "as long as the presumption of *justitia* remains in a man, there remains immense pride, self-trust, smugness. . . . The proclamation of free grace and the forgiveness of sins does not enter his heart and understanding, because that huge rock and solid wall, namely the presumption of *justitia* by which the heart itself is surrounded, prevents this from happening."[25] Beyond the menacing alternatives of despair and smugness lay authentic certainty. "This is the reason why our theology is certain: it snatches us away from ourselves and places us outside ourselves, so that we do not depend on our own strength, conscience, experience, person, or works but depend on that which is outside ourselves, that is, on the promise and truth of God, which cannot deceive."[26]

In the realm of *justitia* as justice, it was equally dangerous to resolve the tension, for there were analogies in the area of social ethics to the despair and the smugness created by an oversimplified theology that refused to live within the paradox. On one side Luther had to respond to the charge that the emphasis of the Reformation on the *justitia* of faith had been responsible for the disruption of the social order because of its unwillingness to accept the medieval compromise. "It is especially saddening," he said, "when we are forced to hear that before the gospel [that is, the Reformation] came everything was tranquil and peaceful, but that since its discovery everything is in an uproar, and . . . that the disobedience of subjects toward their magistrates; sedition, war, pestilence, hunger; the overthrow of states, regions, and kingdoms; sectarianism, scandals, and endless similar evils have all arisen from this teaching."[27] Adjusting the demands of *justitia* to the ambiguity and compromise of historical existence was not the way to live in the tension; for the history of the medieval church proved that lowering the demands only led to further deviation from the norms of *justitia* and finally to moral breakdown, all in the name of regulations that were indeed relatively "useful for external discipline, to keep everything orderly in the churches,"[28] but that had no right to be equated with the absolute requirements of the will of God.

On the other side Luther had to deal with those who felt

able to resolve the tension in the opposite direction by claiming that the compromises and adjustments of relative social *justitia* were a betrayal of the absolute obedience to the will of God required of all men. Viewed in an ultimate way, distinctions of social position among men were, of course, relative, and they did not determine the *justitia* of a man in the sight of God. Nevertheless it was wrong to reject these distinctions, for without them "confusion would result, and all respect and order would disappear."[29] Those who scorned such relative distinctions also spurned the tradition of jurisprudence on the grounds of its pagan origin, urging that civil legislation be replaced by biblical laws. "The political laws of Moses do not apply to us at all," Luther insisted, and "we should not restore them to the courthouse or chain ourselves to them in some superstitious way."[30] At the same time it would not "be a sin if the emperor used some of the civil laws of Moses; in fact, it would be a good idea if he did," but because these laws were reasonable, not because they were biblical.[31] Roman political thought was pagan, to be sure, as were all the "wisdom, power, honorable deeds, outstanding virtues, laws, *justitia,* worship, and religion" of the Greeks and Romans; but "we must not imagine that the Gentiles were simply despisers of honesty and religion, but all the nations scattered all over the world had their own laws, worship, and religion, without which the human race cannot be governed."[32] Hence it was perfectly appropriate to work for *justitia* as justice by means of laws that came from reason rather than from revelation, for *justitia* as justice was the proper realm for reason, whether pagan or Christian.[33]

To avoid both despair and smugness in the realm of faith, *justitia* as righteousness needed the certainty of faith. To avoid the counterparts of these alternatives in the public order, namely, despair and rashness, *justitia* as justice needed the proper mixture of prudence and fortitude—an insight that Luther appears to have learned from Aristotle.[34] "Fortitude," in Luther's definition, was "a steadiness of mind, which does not despair in the midst of adversity but endures bravely and looks for better things. But unless fortitude is directed by prudence, it becomes rashness; on the other hand, unless fortitude is added to prudence, prudence is useless."[35] Resolving the tension in either direction undercut the possibility of attaining that measure of *justitia* as justice to which right reason could attain even in its fallen state.

The Social-Ethical Paralysis of Lutheranism

The temptation of adjusting the absolute demands of *justitia* to the relativities of existence and the temptation of withdrawing from those relativities because they cannot be comformed to the absolute still seem to be the dual forms of evasion of responsibility to which Christian ethics is subject both in its consideration of *justitia* as righteousness and in its striving for *justitia* as justice. Yet Luther's realism about the relation between absolute demand and relative achievement can lead also to another posture, which is neither despair nor smugness, but a special variety of social-ethical paralysis; and this posture has afflicted many of Luther's followers. Whether or not it led to this in Luther's own career and thought is an issue on which much learning and much defensiveness have been expended.[36] But even those who defend his stand in the Peasants' War or his language about the Jews agree that Lutheranism after the Reformation established so placid a *modus vivendi* with the relativities of a proximate social *justitia* that it failed to deal creatively with the ethical crises of modern culture or to relate itself significantly to the movements that have been working for *justitia* in the realm of law and society.[37] It is easy to understand how Luther's recognition of the paradox between *justitia* and *Realpolitik* could lead to the political and social conservatism of Lutheranism both in Europe and in America—once the nerve of Luther's ethic was severed.

That nerve was the hope and courage engendered by faith in the God who demanded an absolute *justitia* but who used the relative *justitia* of man's concrete societies for his own purposes. This hope "arouses the mind to be brave and resolute, so that it dares, endures, and lasts in the midst of evils and looks for better things. . . . It battles with joy and courage in opposition to those great evils."[38] In Luther's ethic—both in his ethical theory and in his actions and decisions—justification by faith did not induce moral paralysis, but the willingness to run risks, to face the possibility of being mistaken, and to let God make the best of the proximate *justitia* to which men could attain. In society God did not require of a man that he do more than he can,[39] not because the demand and the gift of God canceled the structures of social *justitia* and made them meaningless so that it did not matter what men did, but because God was willing and able to use these ambiguous structures and efforts, making up what they lacked. For "God does indeed approve [civil *justitia*], require that it be performed, and offer rewards to it, and to some extent reason is able to perform it."[40] Within their limits, therefore political legislation and other "elements of the world . . . should be held in esteem."[41]

Freed by the doctrine of justification and by this ethical realism from the necessity of adopting an attitude of "all or nothing at all" either about *justitia* as righteousness or about *justitia* as justice, and yet always drawn by the lure of perfect *justitia* in God, the Christian in society, like the Christian in the church, was protected against the self-satisfaction of the moral cynic who finally accepts social injustice as inevitable and against the despair of the crusader who eventually finds that absolute justice is a chimera. "For my *justitia* is not yet perfect. . . . Yet I do not despair on that account."[42] With this insight, the Christian was free to do what he can do, and he was willing to do what he must do; for he lived by the gift of *justitia* as righteousness and lived for the goal of *justitia* as justice. He could collaborate with all those who aimed for this goal, regardless of their relation to *justitia* as righteousness, because he knew that the laws and structures of society "are actually good and useful, but in the proper order and proper place."[43] The true advancement of social *justitia* came not from the idealist who seeks to establish the kingdom of God on earth, nor yet from the cynic who signs an armistice with a morally ambiguous *status quo,* but from the faith-full realist who seeks to move society from the *status quo* of where it is to the ultimate goal of where it ought to be by taking one step at a time toward the proximate goal of where it can be. In the same way, *justitia* as righteousness became concrete neither in the presumption of the self-righteous nor in the despair of the cowardly, but in the courage of the justified, who does all he can because God has already done all he needs. Therefore "the final cause of the obedience of the [divine] law by the righteous is not *justitia* in the sight of God, which is received by faith alone, but the peace of the world."[44] For, as Luther's *Lectures on Genesis* put it, "faith and the Holy Spirit do not corrupt or destroy nature, but heal and restore it after it has been corrupted and destroyed."[45] Or, to paraphrase the axiom of Thomas Aquinas, "*justitia* as righteousness does not abolish *justitia* as justice, but sustains it."[46]

VIII
The Theologian as a Humanistic Scholar

In chapter one we called attention to the close historical connection between Luther's Reformation and the humanistic scholarship of the sixteenth century. The Christian intellectuals who espoused the cause of the Reformation were almost all scholars in the fields that today would be classified as part of the humanities, especially in philology and philosophy. Luther himself would have to be classified as a professor, not of systematic or dogmatic theology but of the Old Testament, and thus as a humanistic scholar.[1] The study of theology is still, to paraphrase Clemenceau's famous remark about war, too important a part of life and culture to be left only to the clergy. Likewise, research in religion is too important a part of scholarly inquiry to be left only to churchly theologians. Such research therefore forms an essential part of the work of the humanities in a secular university. In those cultures and periods of history in which the church has created, nourished, and controlled the university, it could, of course, be assumed that such research was a legitimate part of the university's task. Harvard was established because the founders dreaded "to leave an illiterate ministry to the churches, when our present ministers shall lie in the dust," and Yale was established because it was feared that Harvard was being unfaithful to this religious charter.[2] In fact, most of the private colleges and universities in North America and several of the public institutions as well owe their origin to religious foundations, which regarded religious studies as essential to the university's curriculum and research in religion as basic to its program of scholarship and publication.[3]

The Problem of Objectivity

That assumption can no longer be taken for granted in the academic community. During the nineteenth century, when the title "university" came into general use (Toronto in 1827, Yale in 1887, etc.), the warrant for the inclusion of religion among the humanistic disciplines came under increasingly critical examination. Two of the most noted discussions of the question were prepared by professors at the University of Berlin more than a hundred years apart, Friedrich Schleiermacher and Adolf Harnack.[4] Each of them was the dominant figure in the German Protestant theology of his day; and each sought to defend, in his own highly characteristic fashion, the place of the Christian, specifically Protestant, theological faculty in the university. Despite such eminent advocacy, the propriety of research and teaching in religious studies at the university continues to be a matter of controversy and discussion.[5]

The juxtaposition of Schleiermacher and Harnack in this debate is all the more interesting because of the contrast between the distinctive emphases for which they are known in the history of Christian thought. Schleiermacher, as chapter one has indicated, was the apostle of religious subjectivity, of the primacy of experience, indeed of *Gefühl,* in religion, over against any effort to objectify it in a set of dogmas, in ritual, or in an institution.[6] Harnack, on the other hand, is still spoken of with awe as the high priest of objective historical research, who could assert the right of research in religion to be taken seriously simply by pointing to his own achievements as a scholar, author, and editor.[7] Both Schleiermacher and Harnack, therefore, recognized the centrality of the issue of scholarly objectivity in any consideration of the right of research in religion to belong to the community of humanistic scholarship. As the natural sciences, the humanities, and the social sciences have grown increasingly sophisticated about methodology, defenders of that right have become increasingly concerned, and perforce increasingly modest, about the methods of research proper to research in religious studies.

Even in the universities that continue to carry on such research, there are many professors in other fields who have grave misgivings about the academic propriety and intellectual respectability of such research. Sometimes the quality and the scholarly standards set for this research by some of its devotees seem determined to do everything possible to confirm these misgivings. In the area of religious studies seminars are sometimes offered and dissertations accepted that would be utterly unacceptable in other parts of the university; and the pietist and the secularist, in a strange alliance, will regard this as quite proper, being agreed that faith and learning should be separate. But even research of unquestionable excellence is obliged today to explain why it still belongs in the study of the humanities at a secular university. Most of the objections to it can be summarized under two questions: Can research in religious studies be sufficiently scholarly and objective to warrant certification as a humanistic discipline by the university? And can it be sufficiently disengaged from both the evangelistic and the professional concerns to be a scholarly field among scholarly fields? These are not merely two forms of the same question. But they must be dealt with together, for only when the question of scholarly objectivity has been faced can the implications of research in religion both for the religious life of the university community and for the training of the clergy be addressed.

"To write the history of a religion," wrote Ernest Renan in his *Vie de Jésus,* "it is necessary, first, to have believed it (otherwise we should not be able to understand how it has charmed and satisfied the human conscience); in the second place, to believe it no longer in an absolute manner, for absolute faith is incompatible with sincere history."[8] To be sure, Renan did not specify what mixture of fond memory and cool skepticism was the proper one for the achievement of the desired balance, nor whether the mixture remains the same for an interpreter of Montanism and an interpreter of Roman Catholicism—entirely apart from the question of how one can "have believed" a religious system which has had no adherents for a millennium or more. For that matter, the research that Renan himself carried on does not exemplify any such satisfying balance, unless romantic wistfulness be termed an adequate substitute for commitment and positivism be equated with scholarship. Nevertheless, Renan's methodological prescription does raise the problem of scholarly objectivity in a piquant way and thus may serve as a text for our examination of the problem of objectivity.

The Question of Presuppositions

The attack upon research in religious studies had much of its origin in the heyday of scientism, when it was assumed that because the natural sciences are based upon accurate measurement and upon laboratory experiments that can be verified through repetition, they lead to hypotheses that gradually become conclusions as the evidence accumulates. Thus the methodology of the natural sciences was thought to be objective throughout, because their very principles and procedures screened out the subjectivity of the experimenter and observer.[9] Coinciding as it did with the golden age of historical research in the nineteenth century and with the beginnings of the study of human personality and society toward the end of that century, this dedication to the scientific method had a decisive effect upon the presuppositions of these disciplines as well.[10] Leopold von Ranke's famous dictum about describing history *wie es eigentlich gewesen* has undoubtedly been caricatured by critics. Yet it does bespeak some naïveté about the interaction between the intellect, the will, and the emotions as this affects a man's apprehension and interpretation of facts past or present.[11] The beginnings of the social sciences were equally presumptuous about their objectivity, and perhaps with even less justification.

In the name of the objectivity of the scientific method, research in religious study was denounced as dogmatism, as indoctrination, as the extension of inner feelings and therefore the pursuit of a will-o'-the-wisp which was by definition unverifiable. The notorious disagreements of theologians over the correct interpretation of texts in the Bible became proof that an exegete finds in Scripture whatever meaning he wants to find and that there is no external curb upon this caprice. Similarly, the quarrels—for example, between the authors of the Magdeburg *Centuries* and Caesar Baronius[12]—over the *testimonia patrum* and the use of Christian antiquities as a weapon in interconfessional polemics seemed to show that church history is different from other history in degree if not actually in kind, simply because the church historian has such a stake in the outcome of his researches. (It should probably be added that Protestant church historians have been as ready to apply this criticism to their Roman Catholic colleagues as have secular historians to regard it as a characteristic of all church history.)[13] Because research in religion thus was lacking in objective verifiability and because there were as many opinions as there were teachers, it could not claim to belong in the community of humanistic scholarship but had to be relegated to the area of private judgment and personal taste.

This situation has been drastically revised—not because of a sudden upsurge of piety among humanistic scholars but because of a growing recognition that there is no such thing as an uninterpreted fact and that therefore an exegesis free of presuppositions is impossible, not only for the student of Isaiah but also for the researcher into fossils or the historian of Latin literature. As a result of the work of Collingwood, Croce, Cochrane, and many other historians and philosophers, everyone has come to agree that the problem of objectivity and presupposition is not peculiar to the field of religion;[14] nor is it, at least in the modern world, most vexing there. The criticisms just recited have combined with the history of critical thought within the religious traditions to make the student of religious history and phenomena acutely aware of the question. Consequently, one difference between many "secular" scholars in the humanities and their colleagues in religious studies has come to be that the students of religious ideas and institutions are both more aware and more explicit about their "position" than are many of their colleagues. The most basic problem is not the presence of presuppositions that may color one's judgment; it is the awareness of these presuppositions, the ability to deal with them methodologically, and the effect they may have on one's capacity to attend to the uniqueness of an alien system or doctrine. Some sets of presuppositions—for example, certain species of contemporary existentialism—may shut one off so completely from anything external or past or foreign that one has, in Harnack's phrase, virtually no antenna.[15] The presence of such presuppositions would constitute a valid ground for objection to a scholar, not because of the correctness or incorrectness of the theological position itself but because of its effect on his capacity for research. But this would be true of other humanistic disciplines as well as of religious studies.

The Variety of Religious Studies

It is essential to keep in mind, when speaking about research in religious studies, that such research includes a range of interests and scholarly areas across a large part of the humanities. Perhaps the most nearly analogous situation is that of a department of history, where an Egyptologist and a student of international relations since World War II are both called historians. Of course, with increasing specialization such range is beginning to characterize most of the departments in the university, with a consequent breakdown of communication within the disciplines that used to take place only between the disciplines. Departments are now clusters of subdepartments, each with its own data and methods. Yet the sheer weight of age and tradition forces the study of religion into an acceptance of such a pluralism of fields and tasks.

This pluralism has special relevance for the problem of scholarly objectivity. Both the case for objectivity and the very definition of it will be different in the different subfields of religious studies. There are certainly some areas of research in religious studies upon whose scientific chastity no other scholar, or at least no other humanist, would cast any aspersions. Perhaps the best illustration is the textual criticism of the New Testament, in relation to the methods of textual criticism as applied to other bodies of literature. From its beginnings in the work of the humanists, especially Erasmus, the textual criticism of the New Testament has developed in close conjunction with classical scholarship.[16] Indeed, many of the methods and principles we now apply to determine the best possible reading originated with the textual critics of the New Testament. In the eighteenth century Johann Albrecht Bengel set down the principle that in a conflict between two equally attested readings one should prefer the one that is harder to explain, since a later transcriber would be more likely to simplify the text with the thought of correcting it than to complicate it.[17] This principle, when applied with imagination and discernment, is still valid both in the study of the Bible and in humanistic scholarship generally. And therefore a student of Elizabethan literature whose own scholarly career depends upon the work of the textual critic of the

First Folio with variations is obligated to accord a place in humanistic scholarship to the textual criticism of the New Testament, whose critical apparatus represents many centuries of meticulous scholarly work.

Nevertheless, although the textual criticism of the New Testament deals with a religious text, it seems to be one of the least religious fields in religious studies. Research in religious studies would then seem to be justified as a humanistic discipline to the extent that it forswore its interest in religion. For there are areas of religious study and ways of working in them that are so wrapped up in normative judgments that no one in the public realm can evaluate them, for example, fields like dogmatic and moral theology. These are the truly troublesome areas, for they are also the ones that are most explicitly "religious" or at least the most churchly. Eliminating these areas a priori would be a draconian solution to the problem of objectivity and would run the danger of trivializing research in religious studies by permitting it to do only those tasks about whose scholarly results no humanistic scholar, inside or outside the churches, will be disturbed.

Do such studies as moral and dogmatic theology deserve the name "research" as this name is understood by the university? They do—or more accurately, they can—provided that there is a major component of scholarship in them that can be validated according to publicly verifiable procedures of disciplined study. Dogmatic theology, for example, has usually been shaped by biblical, historical, or philosophical study, or by some combination of two or of all three of these. Which of the three ought to play which role in dogmatic theology is a matter of much controversy among the theologians and between the churches, but each of the three components is a humanistic discipline whose materials and methods are accessible to any scholar with the necessary technical and linguistic equipment. On the basis of this criterion there are some kinds of Christian dogmatics that would qualify as legitimate areas of research and some kinds that would not. Most of those that would not, to be honest, are those that would not want to and would, in fact, glory in their very exclusion. For that matter, some ways of doing biblical exegesis would pass muster, while others would not; and even some ways of church history would certainly be ruled out. Most theologians who are also concerned about humanistic scholarship probably believe that this same criterion applies to any teaching and writing in religious studies, whether in the secular university or in a school directly under the church. But humanistic scholarship has its own reasons for insisting on this criterion, and the reasons are sound.

The Case for General Education

The case for religious studies within the humanities is part of the case for general education and for its bearing upon all forms of scholarship. Many a humanistic scholar has discovered that the decisive component in truly significant research is frequently the factor that could not have been supplied by any numbers of hours of further investigation but only by a close and continuing acquaintance with the best in the entire heritage of humanistic thought.

Such a prejudice in favor of general education becomes most evident at the level of undergraduate teaching, but it is no less relevant to scholarship. For the presence of presuppositions in the work of the scholar or graduate student is an advantage rather than a disadvantage, simply because it is one of the most effective ways of relating the specialization of the scholar to the general issues of education, and indeed of humanity, with which he is obliged to deal. When Anders Nygren speaks of "the role of the self-evident in history," he is referring to those concepts and convictions about which a writer does not speak because he does not have to, but into which the historian must seek to penetrate because he cannot understand what the author says unless he grasps also what the author means without saying it.[18] It is to these self-evident axioms of our own thought and work that we are driven when the question of objectivity and presupposition compels us to reflect on our own discipline and its hidden assumptions. When we thus face the challenge of presuppositions squarely, we are enabled to come at general education not before our specialization or around it, but through it. There are philosophers who argue that the scholar must clarify his presuppositions before he begins his research, for otherwise his research will be lacking in intellectual integrity.[19] But as the process of self-examination is more fruitful when one has acquired a self to examine, so the examination of presuppositions requires some measure of competence and achievement in a scholarly discipline.

When a scholar sounds the depths of his own discipline and begins to see what binds it to others and what makes it distinctive, he simultaneously addresses the question of general education and refines his own disciplines. Any university that attempts to undertake this assignment without paying attention to religious studies is cutting itself off from one of the richest resources available to it for this very quest. The scholarly subject matter of religious studies is inevitably broader than its administrative province in any modern university. One thinks, for example, of the virtual monopoly which anthropologists and social psychologists have acquired in the area of primitive religion, or of the dominance of political and literary historians in the field of Puritan studies.[20] Throughout the humanities, then, there are scholars dealing with data that would be a proper subject for research in religious studies, and this is as it should be. But this distribution of research in religious studies does provide a setting for a university-wide consideration of the presuppositions of general education, in which research in religious studies may render a service to the rest of the university precisely because of its self-consciousness about the relation between fact and interpretation. Research in religious studies must, in turn, be informed and called to account by such an exchange with the methods and materials of its sister disciplines, as indeed it has been over and over again.

The Problem of Professional Education

Within the context of these observations on the problem of objectivity in research on religion we may now consider the bearing of such research on the professional education of the clergy. The study of theology by the present and future servants of the church has always sought a structure for its work and a definition for its task that would keep it related responsibly to the empirical church and yet keep it free to do its work. The reorganization of the Continental and British universities during the Renaissance and Reformation accorded an honored and secure place to professors of divinity;[21] and if we are to judge by the scholarly fruits, the habilitation of theological research as a humanistic discipline within the university has unquestionably been a blessing for the disciplined study of theology and thus for the education of the clergy. But it has not been an unmixed blessing. In the eighteenth century the evangelical revival in Great Britain and Pietism on the Continent were agreed that academic theology had been so alienated from the church that the professors of divinity at the universities were not fit to teach the preachers of the gospel.[22] Shaped as they were by this mood of evangelicalism and Pietism, many of the Protestants who came to Canada and the United States were determined that their ministers would be trained in an atmosphere where true piety and sound learning were properly mixed. As a result most of the clergy in both these countries are educated in schools that are directly responsible to the boards of some denomination.[23]

Yet this method of professional education has often been

impoverished because of its exclusive preoccupation with the church at the expense of the university. The education of the clergy needs to be tied to the churches, but it also needs to feel the scholarly pressure that only the university can supply. As both a Reformer and a humanistic scholar Luther recognized the liberating value of this pressure in helping to make him a Reformer: "I never wanted to do it, and I do not want to do it now. I was forced and driven into this position in the first place when I became a Doctor of Theology. As a Doctor in a general free university, I began . . . to do what such a Doctor is sworn to do, expounding the Scriptures for all the world and teaching everybody. Once in this position, I have had to stay in it, and I cannot give it up or leave it with a good conscience. . . . For what I began as a Doctor . . . I must truly confess to the end of my life."[24] Luther's position as a Doctor of Theology in the university bound him to the church, yet it gave him the freedom he needed to serve the church as an "obedient rebel."[25] What the American and Canadian churches continue to need is to have at least some of the research in religious studies carried on by those who are, as Luther was, "Doctors in a general free university"—willing to act responsibly, able to act freely. Only such research will be able to do for the churches what the churches need but often cannot or will not do for themselves. And only as a result of such research will the ministers of those churches receive an education instead of merely a training.

Both for theological study itself and for humanistic scholarship generally there is much to be gained from the effort to rehabilitate religious studies within the humanities. The implications of much of the material we have examined in both parts of this book would seem to point in that direction, both negatively and positively. For where the intellectual exchange between theology and the humanities has been lost, both have been impoverished by being able to avoid the kind of probing that only such exchange can foster. The "Christian intellectual" with whose portrait these essays have been dealing was, in the Reformation, a Christian humanist—regardless of the academic discipline or profession in which he worked. This was true, for example, of Kepler. The relation between Christian thought and "natural philosophy," considered in earlier chapters, likewise moves toward this conclusion. In the final chapter we shall deal with the relation between the community of scholarship and the community of faith.

IX
The Church and the Christian Intellectual

As we have had occasion to observe—at considerable length in chapter one, briefly in chapter eight—the work of the Christian intellectual has often created suspicion and even alienation between him and the Christian community. The earliest defenders of Christian orthodoxy felt obliged to attack "the vaunting of the so-called intellectuals";[1] and Origen, who deserves the title "Christian intellectual" if anyone does, has been accused repeatedly of intellectual pride and disobedience to the church.[2] Thus the Christian intellectual is frequently on the defensive not only against other intellectuals but also against other Christians. If there is to be a renewal of Christian intellectual life, nourished by the heritage of the Reformation, the relation of the Christian intellectual to the church will have to be rethought, and the ecclesiastical and theological obstacles to such renewal will have to be faced.

Suspicion of the Elite

The most formidable theological and ecclesiastical obstacle to the renewal of Christian intellectual life, especially in America, is a curious alliance between the secular suspicion of an elite that has been characteristic of much of American life and a distorted interpretation of the Reformation doctrine of the universal priesthood of all believers. As America, where, in Tocqueville's phrase, "a middling standard is fixed . . . for human knowledge,"[3] represents a repudiation of the aristocratic structures and traditions of old Europe, so Protestantism is represented as a repudiation of the hierarchical structures and traditions of medieval Catholicism. The result of this blending is an equalitarianism that regards the emphasis on scholarly merit and intellectual competence as dangerous and that therefore prefers the schooling of the many to the educating of the few.

Any discussion of the cultivation of scholarship and intellectual excellence must come to terms with the problems and risks involved in the emphasis on an intellectual elite. It summons up the vision of a culture where the specialists in various intellectual disciplines are so preoccupied with their own research that the appearance of demonic forces in the culture escapes their notice or does not seem to be their concern. The record of the performance of the German universities in the years of the rise of Fascism is not encouraging to anyone who is himself a research scholar and who believes in a renewed stress upon excellence and quality. It should, of course, be added that the performance of the churches, both Protestant and Roman Catholic, also left a great deal to be desired, as a recent study by Guenter Lewy on Roman Catholicism and several shorter studies on Protestantism have begun to make clear.[4] Nevertheless, if we are to deal frankly with the role of the intellectual, we must address the fundamental problem raised by this objection. As we shall point out a little later, the objection itself is a sound one, and it introduces a factor into the definition of excellence and quality which is frequently ignored by those whose approach to intellectual development is a purely technical one.

Nevertheless the grounds on which this objection is usually based—the alliance between American equalitarianism and the pietistic interpretation of the universal priesthood of believers—must be examined very critically. For both the American stress upon equal rights and the Protestant doctrine of the essential equality of all men before God are, in their more profound sense, a resource for the fullest possible development of the talents and potential of all men rather than for the common effort to cut everyone down to size. Theologically speaking, the essential corollary of the doctrine of the universal priesthood of believers is the Reformation doctrine of vocation, which declares that the fullest possible actualization of the potential in the talents and endowments of each individual is not merely a means of fulfilling personal ambition but an instrument for obeying and glorifying God.[5] Similarly the American doctrine of equal rights dare not be permitted to imply that when intellectual performance does not meet standards, standards should be adjusted to performance, but it must be taken with utmost seriousness as a statement of the principle, also enunciated by Tocqueville, "that although the capacities of men are different, as the Creator intended they should be, the means that Americans find for putting them to use are equal."[6] Unless the colleges and universities of the United States are able to make this fundamental distinction, democracy will come to mean, as its critics have said, a sharing of mediocrity. And unless the colleges and universities of the church develop the doctrine of vocation as profoundly as they have permitted themselves to be shaped by a distorted doctrine of the universal priesthood, they, too, will move increasingly toward a custodial function in the life and thought of the youth of the church.

This requires some basic research, both historical and theological, into the fuller implications of the doctrines which Americans affirm as well as of the doctrines which evangelical Christians confess. It has only been in our own century, for example, that Luther's doctrine of the calling has become an object of special study by German, Swedish, and American scholars.[7] Similarly it has only been in the last few decades that American historians and political thinkers have examined the roots of anti-intellectualism in American history. The implications of these historical and theological studies for the task of the Christian intellectual are only now being faced.[8] At this point, as at so many others, secular educational thought has drawn implications from the facts which should have been drawn by the schools of the church much earlier from their own fundamental convictions.

The Peril of Gnosticism

A second obstacle to the renewal of Christian intellectual life is the church's fundamental suspicion of Gnosticism. Gnosticism divided men according to their ability to perceive the deeper mysteries of the faith. This stratification of men into three classes—the spiritual, the psychic, and the carnal—was used as the basis for the claim that the authority of Scripture and of the apostolic tradition applied only to the lower class of men. The truly spiritual man, as I Cor. 2 : 15 had said, judges all but is himself judged by none. From this the Gnostics drew the conclusion that the spiritual man, that is to say the true Gnostic, was above both the doctrinal and the moral standards of orthodox Christianity.[9]

In opposition to this notion, wherever and whenever it has appeared in Christian history, the church has insisted upon the totality of the lordship of Christ, regardless of the intellectual or personal endowments of any man. Or, to put it in the words of Irenaeus, "it does not follow because men are endowed with greater and less degrees of intelligence, that they should therefore change the subject matter of the faith itself."[10] Irenaeus recognized the temptation to intellectual *hybris* in the Gnostic claims, and he sought to erect a protecting wall against this *hybris* in his insistence on the apostolic tradition. Repeatedly in Christian history since, such Gnostic notions have reappeared, and each time the church has been obliged to reassert the position of Irenaeus. But having said that, one must immediately go on to say that the church has also frequently asserted this position against not intellectual *hybris* but intellectual responsibility. The sound insight of Irenaeus, that the essential content of the Christian message is not negotiable regardless of the level of one's intellectual attainment, quickly and easily becomes, in the hands of an inquisitor, a way of branding every Christian intellectual a Gnostic. Perhaps the outstanding instance of this in the ancient church was the condemnation of Origen. In the past century and a half theologians who have dared to apply the methods of historical scholarship to the study of Bible and tradition have been joined by natural scientists who have dared to examine the implications of their research; together these two groups of scholars have borne the brunt of attacks by the inquisitors, as Part One of this book has shown.

If Christian intellectuals who stand in the tradition of the Reformation intend to reassert the place of the life of the mind in the church, they will have to come to terms both with the peril of Gnosticism and with the deeper implications of anti-Gnostic thought. For it certainly must be admitted that some forms of the call to excellence in the intellectual community have a distinct echo of Gnosticism in them, and Christians who participate in this call must be more sensitive to the dangers than many of them have been. There are theological and intellectual resources both in the teachings of the church and in the American tradition for avoiding this pitfall, but it is dismaying to observe the ease with which the spokesmen for the empirical church can use this pitfall as an excuse to attack all reflective and critical thinking.

The Need for Ministers

A third obstacle to the emphasis on intellectual quality in the church and in its schools is the responsibility they carry for the training of the professional servants of the church, especially for the education of the church's clergy. This is, to be sure, a matter of considerable delicacy, and one on which it is possible to speak quite irresponsibly. Nevertheless a refusal to face the evident trends and tendencies in the churches will jeopardize the opportunity to do anything at all about the level of intellectual life and responsibility in the church.

As a result of several sensationalistic articles in the popular press during the past several years, the spokesmen for the church have developed a defensive interpretation of trends in the recruitment, training, and morale of the Protestant clergy. When magazine articles profess to describe a large incidence of mental breakdown, moral collapse, and professional dereliction among Protestant ministers, the journals of the church quite understandably point to the continued tradition of dedicated service and personal commitment among Protestant clergy. Valid though this response may be, it may blind one to a subtler but more pervasive problem that does in fact exist within the churches. Despite the high intellectual quality of many of the young men going into the ministry of the Protestant churches, the fact remains that there are still entirely too many students of marginal intellectual capacity being admitted to and graduated from the seminaries of the church, and that the church seems willing, if not indeed determined, to encourage and accept such students for the ranks of its clergy.[11]

In part, of course, this is a symptom of an entire shift in our culture. The natural sciences are recruiting students at an ever earlier age, as indeed they must because of the immense amount of technical training that a student must have to do research and teaching in the natural sciences. The social sciences and especially the humanities frequently are obliged to do their recruiting much later. In fact, the humanities are obliged, not only by their position in the culture but by their very nature, to recruit students at a later age than the natural sciences do. As the preceding chapter has pointed out, the study of religion, whether as an academic subject or as a preparation for professional service in the church, no longer occupies the position it once did. The net result is that in all too many places the ministry of the church is chosen by those who have remained after the natural sciences, the social sciences, and the other branches of the humanities have made their appeal. Even within the area of religious study and service, moreover, a career of teaching and research is frequently regarded as preferable to the ministry of preaching and pastoral work.[12]

In many ways, of course, this problem involves not primarily the definition of the role of the Christian intellectual but the understanding of the task of the Christian minister. When practical men in the church resist the raising of intellectual standards for the clergy on these grounds, it does not help to ignore the real urgency of their situation. The church truly is caught at many places in the world between a desperate need for hands and voices, on the one hand, and the rising standards and demands of an increasingly technological society. It is irresponsible to issue a call for academic excellence in indifference to this predicament.

But serious examination of the task of the church in Western society does not seem to substantiate the claim that the intellectual and academic standards applied to the ministry of the Reformation churches in their "classic age" must now be lowered to take account of the new situation. In the age of the Reformation "it was believed that a humanistically and theologically trained minister who had been taught how to interpret the Bible would effectively lead the common people in Christian faith and life, chiefly through his preaching and teaching";[13] it is difficult to understand the argument of those who claim that for the training of the ministry in the twentieth century a shorter course of study is not only permissible but preferable. Students of the history and present sociological situation of the Protestant churches in America have frequently pointed to the proliferation of small and competing congregations throughout those areas of the country where Protestantism is dominant.[14] The result of this proliferation is, among other things, a highly uneconomic use of ministerial resources. Such a use of ministers, which has its parallel in the employment of ministers for essentially secular tasks in the administrative and bureaucratic structures of the denominations, can be justified only on the grounds that the waste of manpower and training involved in such a table of organization does not really represent the diversion of highly trained personnel from other positions but is, realistically speaking, the best possible use of their abilities.

Now any such statistical or quantitative formulation of the needs and prospects is, of course, a vast oversimplification. The factors of Christian formation[15] (to use the familiar Roman Catholic term), of devotion and dedication, and of the support granted to the minister by the entire witness and work of the congregation would all have to be considered much more carefully before any conclusions were drawn. In every period of the church's history there have been Christian pastors whose spiritual power, purity of character, and depth of commitment have enabled them to overcome the handicaps of quite ordinary intellectual equipment and meager academic training. But the task of interpreting and proclaiming the word of God and of relating its promises and imperatives to the genuine alternatives of contemporary life cannot be left to the caprices of individual whim, regardless of how committed it may be.

Since our concern in this volume is with the intellectual life of all Christians rather than merely with that of the clergy, the argument against intellectual quality on the grounds of the church's need for professional servants may be reversed. The only way an inadequately trained clergyman can function in today's society is with the support and counsel of intellectual laymen. A community of Christian intellectuals must be a place where the intellectual demands of the Christian life are voiced, where the doubts and challenges of contemporary culture are considered seriously, and where the alternative solutions for the problem of Christian faith in modern thought are discussed openly and freely. There would appear to be few better contexts for the clergy of the church to develop than in the midst of such a free flow of ideas and questions. Does anyone seriously argue that in the church of the future we can afford to have a highly trained laity and a poorly trained ministry, or that the intellectual demands of being a Christian clergyman in the last third of this century are less rigorous than they have been in previous times or than they will be for Christian laymen?

The Quality of Life

In spite of these formidable obstacles the renewal of the life of the mind in the churches can draw upon the resources of the Christian heritage for special insight into the problems and the promises of intellectual pursuits. One such insight is that the primary concern of the cultivation of the mind is the quality of a life, not merely the earning of a living. For generations of immigrants to the United States intellectual development has been an escalator to social and economic success. Many a leader of American society is what he is because his hard-working parents were determined that his lot in the world must be better than theirs. In the same way the heroic struggle of the American Negro to achieve at last the rights that have been theoretically his for a century is properly concentrated upon the schools, for the way to genuine emancipation lies through education. And those who are blocking the path to emancipation recognize correctly that once they lose control of their discriminatory school systems and colleges, their whole wretched cause is doomed. The improvement of the intellect is still the best way for individuals or groups to raise their social standing and their income.

Yet professional training and schooling for success can be futile and even demonic unless they are based upon that fullness of mind and wholeness of vision which are the results of truly humane learning. As we noted earlier, the twentieth century has learned to be afraid of any university system that can train specialists without making them citizens of the *universitas,* the universal realm of humane thought and discourse. In opposition to such a system the Christian intellectual has a special responsibility to cultivate a depth that is more than specialization and a breadth that is more than dilettantism. The Christian intellectual is the natural ally of those who contend that a basic part of the response to technology must be increased study of the liberal and liberating arts. The understanding of man summarized in chapter six implies that the only specialist who can be trusted is one who has first learned to think clearly about the ultimate question of what it means to be human. For a man's life does not consist in the abundance of the things which he possesses, nor yet in the techniques he has learned for acquiring them, but in the qualities of mind and spirit that enable him to survive both adversity and prosperity—qualities that spring from the twin sources of Christian thought and a humanistic education. Only from such an education can come the respect for man and his worth upon which Western culture is founded. Only where a man is respected as an end in himself rather than a means can the specialization of the technician be rescued from manipulation. Therefore the primary aim of intellectual growth ought to be this quality of life.

To make its special contribution to this cause, the church will have to formulate a Christian doctrine of enjoyment. The opening question of *The Shorter Catechism* was: "What is the chief end of man? To glorify God and to enjoy him for ever."[16] The enjoyment of God, the *fruitio Dei* of which Augustine wrote,[17] is a direct corollary of central Christian dogmas like the Trinity and is a special motif of the book of Psalms. It means that a basic element of the life in God is the joyful sharing in the goodness of the world and in the richness of what man has been able to discover and to dream. Students are being swindled out of their inheritance if they are permitted to graduate from college or university without knowing the zest of such enjoyment, regardless of how they eventually earn their livings. As we have had occasion to note before, the Christian intellectual is not alone in his dedication to this aim. Sometimes, in fact, the sons of this world are wiser in their own generation than the sons of light, so that the Christian intellectual has had to relearn this ancient Christian truth from nonchurchly sources.

Outgrowing One's Teachers

Few tyrannies are more insidious than that of a teacher who is interested in disciples rather than pupils, who seeks to be imitated rather than transcended, and who is so sure of the correctness of his ideas that he can evaluate all his students on the basis of their obedience to his opinions rather than on the basis of their judgment and maturity. The history of Christian theology has not lacked for such teachers, who have compounded the tyranny by identifying their notions with the word of God and thus equating their authority with the sovereignty of God. Yet no field of study is free of this temptation, and no intellectual community can afford to relent in its vigil against the tyranny of the pedagogue.

The Christian intellectual has a special reason to demand that a teacher point beyond himself, as chapter one has suggested. Because only "one is our Master, even Christ" (Matt. 23 : 8) and all others are merely his disciples, or at least try to be, no teacher has the right to usurp that prerogative. Therefore Luther stoutly resisted the tendency of his followers to call themselves "Lutheran," but the tendency prevailed.[18] In Christian thought there is, of course, a recognition of the fundamental distinction between the teacher and the learner.

As we noted earlier in this chapter, Christian community does not imply the sort of fuzzy-minded equalitarianism that dissolves the very structure of the educational process for the sake of "chumminess." But Christian community does mean that the distinction between the teacher and the learner, although necessary, is finally relative under the kingship of him who is Lord of all; as we noted in chapter seven, other such distinctions must also be viewed as both necessary and relative.[19] This means that the teacher teaches as one who goes on studying. He inducts the novice into the community of thought and inquiry so that the pupil may go on to be a student and begin studying for himself.

Because it is the function of the teacher to make his students outgrow him, it follows that Jesus Christ cannot be merely a teacher.[20] For the definition of Christian maturity is growth into Christ, to the measure of the stature of his fullness. Therefore he is the Lord and the Saviour, because he has reconciled the world to the Father and by the gift of his Spirit he incorporates men into himself through the church, which is the fullness of him who fills all in all. Those who live in that church are members one of another, different though their functions may be; but only he is the head of the body, from whom the members, individually and together, receive their direction. A teacher must work to obliterate himself; Christ is he through whom men are united with the Father, and therefore he is more than a teacher. The Christian intellectual, then, lives under the lordship of Christ, in whose service is perfect freedom. Thus the Christian intellectual is set free from the onerous responsibility of being right every time. It is no tragedy for a teacher to be mistaken. It is a tragedy if he is so afraid of being mistaken that he refuses to take risks, or if he imagines that his office has endowed him with infallibility. In chapter seven we have drawn some of the implications of Luther's doctrine of justification for such a view of risk taking.[21]

The Renewal of Tradition

Whatever else an education ought to do, it should provide one with a sophisticated perspective on his own time and culture. It should teach him to appreciate what he has, but to put it into context, especially into the context of the past. Sophistication is usually defined as the very antithesis of tradition. When this happens, students are prevented from developing the style of the truly educated man, which can come only through a renewal of tradition. They have been deprived of the great discovery that the past and the present, far from being opposites, actually require each other for completeness. The thrill of that discovery has perhaps never been stated as persuasively as by Gilbert Chesterton.[22]

Seen in this relation to the modern world, tradition is a power for liberation, setting one free from the dictatorship of the claim that his own time or culture or school is the goal toward which history has been moving. For the Christian intellectual this renewal of tradition is the only way to find an intelligible connection between Christian thought and both "natural philosophy" and the "humanities." Tradition in this sense is the very opposite of the traditionalism that uses the dead theories of the past as a club to beat down all creativity in the present. Authentic tradition is a function of the critical memory and the creative imagination. It is an organism getting out of itself in order to see itself. Only that man is truly educated who has learned this art. Only that man is a Christian intellectual who protects himself against both traditionalism and iconoclasm through the renewal of the tradition of Christian faith, thought, worship, and service. The Christian intellectual can perform no more vital service for both the church and the intellectual community than to show in his concrete life that such a renewal of tradition is the indispensable counterpart of both reflective thought and scientific inquiry.

That renewal of tradition was the very assignment that the Reformation of the sixteenth century set for itself. Far from being dedicated to the overthrow of the centuries of Christian heritage, Luther and his followers pledged their loyalty to all that was noble and Christian in the Catholic substance of the tradition—including those noble things that had been taken up into the tradition from the humanities. The Christian intellectuals of the Reformation carried Homer in one hand and the epistles of Paul in the other, as we noted at the very beginning of this book. They were persuaded that both the church and the culture of the sixteenth century needed the renewing power of this entire spiritual and intellectual heritage. Both the church and the culture of the twentieth century require nothing less.

Notes

Abbreviations in Notes

BC *The Book of Concord,* tr. by Theodore G. Tappert, Jaroslav Pelikan, Robert H. Fischer, and Arthur C. Piepkorn. Philadelphia, 1959.

Bek. *Die Bekenntnisschriften der evangelisch-lutherischen Kirche.* 2nd ed., Göttingen, 1952.

LW *Luther's Works* (American Ed.), eds. Jaroslav Pelikan and Helmut T. Lehmann. St. Louis and Philadelphia, 1955–.

WA *D. Martin Luthers Werke.* Weimar, 1883–. *Tischreden* (*WA Ti*). *Deutsche Bibel* (*WA, DB*).

Chapter I The Christian Intellectual on the Defensive

1 Philip Melanchthon, "De corrigendis adolescentiae studiis," *Melanchthons Werke in Auswahl,* eds. Robert Stupperich et al., III (Gütersloh, 1961), 40, 41. Cf. the comments of Heinrich Bornkamm, *Das Jahrhundert der Reformation: Gestalten und Kräfte* (Göttingen, 1961), p. 57.

2 Cf. George Huntston Williams, *The Radical Reformation* (Philadelphia, 1962), "Introduction," p. xxiv.

3 *Dissonant Voices in Soviet Literature,* eds. Patricia Blake and Max Hayward (New York, 1964), p. xii; Paul Valéry, *The Outlook for Intelligence* (Eng. tr. New York, 1963), p. 80; James Reston, "Our History Suggests a Remedy," *The National Purpose* (New York, 1960), p. 116; Hans J. Morgenthau, *The Purpose of American Politics* (New York, 1964), p. 68; Andrew Sinclair, *Era of Excess: A Social History of the Prohibition Movement* (New York, 1964), p.

332; Ludwig von Mises, *The Anti-Capitalist Mentality* (Princeton, 1956), p. 107; David Riesman and Nathan Glazer, "The Intellectuals and the Discontented Classes," *The Radical Right,* ed. Daniel Bell (New York, 1964), pp. 105–159; John Gunther, *The Lost City* (New York, 1964), p. 533.

[4] *Über die Religion: Reden an die Gebildeten unter ihren Verächtern* was first published anonymously in 1799; a second and revised edition appeared in 1806; a third with further revisions came out in 1821. These three editions have been collated in the standard critical edition: Friedrich Schleiermacher, *Reden über die Religion,* ed. G. Ch. Bernard Pünjer (Braunschweig, 1879). The standard English translation is: *On Religion: Speeches to Its Cultured Despisers,* tr. John Oman, with an introduction by Rudolf Otto (repr. New York, 1958); Professor Pauck's comments appear on the back cover of this edition. Oman's translation is based upon the text of 1821, without any indication of changes from the earlier editions. In my footnotes I shall refer to the Pünjer edition as *Reden,* with a superscript numeral to indicate the edition; I shall follow this with a reference to the English translation in parentheses (*ET*). Wherever possible, I have adhered to the Oman translation, altering it only for the sake of accuracy or clarity.

[5] *Reden*^{1}, p. 3 (*ET* 2). See Wilhelm Dilthey, *Leben Schleiermachers,* I, ed. Hermann Mulert (Berlin and Leipzig, 1922), 407–419. *Reden*^{3}, p. 206 (*ET* 170).

[6] *Reden*^{2}, pp. 2–3 (*ET* 2). *Reden*^{1}, p. 148 (*ET* 119); p. 184 (*ET* 151). See the brief but helpful comments of Paul Seifert, *Die Theologie des jungen Schleiermacher* (Gütersloh, 1960), pp. 50–53.

[7] *Reden*^{1}, p. 174 (*ET* 141).

[8] See the discussion of Chrysostomus Baur, *John Chrysostom and his Time,* tr. Sr. M. Gonzaga, I (Westminster, Md., 1959), 206–258; John Knox, *The Early Church and the Coming Great Church* (New York and Nashville, 1955), pp. 97–100.

[9] *Reden*^{2}, p. 60 (*ET* 49–50); p. 47 (*ET* 36); p 72 (*ET* 58). *Reden*^{1}, pp. 243–244 (*ET* 214); cf. Otto Ritschl, "Das Verhältnis von Empirie und Spekulation in Schleiermachers Reden über die Religion," *Schleiermachers Stellung zum Christentum in seinen Reden über die Religion* (Gotha, 1888), pp. 29–44. *Reden*^{1}, p. 274 (*ET* 237).

[10] Albrecht Ritschl could even speak of "the general science of religion (*die allgemeine Religionswissenschaft*), which was established by Scheiermacher's *Reden.*" *Schleiermachers Reden über die Religion und ihre Nachwirkungen auf die evangelische Kirche Deutschlands* (Bonn, 1874), p. 62. On the apologists, cf. *Reden*^{1}, pp.

120–133 (*ET* 92–101); p. 12 (*ET* 9); pp. 115–117 (*ET* 88–90); also Basil Willey, *The Seventeenth Century Background* (New York, 1953).

[11] *Reden*[1], p. 43 (*ET* 33). Anton Hammer, *Die erkenntnistheoretische Bedeutung des gefühlmässigen Erfassens bei Schleiermacher* (Freiburg, 1934), is an attempt to gauge the epistemological role of *Gefühl* and to distinguish it from mere feeling-as-emotion. A similar attempt, which, although it concentrates upon the *Glaubenslehre*, is relevant also to the *Reden*, is F. Siegmund-Schultze, *Schleiermachers Psychologie in ihrer Bedeutung für die Glaubenslehre* (Tübingen, 1913), pp. 131–210.

[12] *Reden*[2], pp. 102–103 (*ET* 80); *Reden*[1], p. 274 (*ET* 237). Cf. Hermann Süskind, *Christentum und Geschichte bei Schleiermacher*, I (Tübingen, 1911).

[13] *Reden*[1], p. 28 (*ET* 21).

[14] *Reden*[1], p. 300 (*ET* 267); *Reden*[1], p. 107 (*ET* 83). See Holger Samson, *Die Kirche als Grundbegriff der theologischen Ethik Schleiermachers* (Zürich, 1958).

[15] In my *From Luther to Kierkegaard* (St. Louis, 1950), pp. 109–112, my interpretation of Schleiermacher was deeply influenced by Emil Brunner, *Die Mystik und das Wort* (Tübingen, 1924), and therefore I made the aesthetic element less ambiguous than it is in fact, at least in Schleiermacher's mature system. I have commented on this in my introduction to the paperback edition (St. Louis, 1963).

[16] *Reden*[2], p. 171 (*ET* 138–139); p. 114 (*ET* 87), where the first edition had "virtuosity" instead of "special calling."

[17] *Reden*[1], p. 68 (*ET* 55); *Reden*[3], p. 304 (*ET* 272); p. 30 (*ET* 23); *Reden*[2], p. 13 (*ET* 10); p. 199 (*ET* 164), where the first edition has "virtuosoes" for "accomplished in religion."

[18] *Reden*[3], p. 23 (*ET* 17). Friedrich Schleiermacher, *Der christliche Glaube nach den Grundsätzen der evangelischen Kirche im Zusammenhange dargestellt*, ed. Martin Redeker (7th edn., Berlin, 1960), I, 148–154. *Schleiermachers Sendschreiben über seine Glaubenslehre an Lücke*, ed. Hermann Mulert (Giessen, 1908). *Reden*[1], p. 281 (*ET* 244).

[19] *Reden*[1], p. 95 (*ET* 73); *Reden*[2], p. 85 (*ET* 65); *Reden*[3], p. 162 (*ET* 131).

[20] *Reden*[2], p. 16 (*ET* 12–13).

[21] *Der christliche Glaube*, II, 105–136 (Theses 102–104).

[22] *Reden*[1], p. 4 (*ET* 3); p. 185 (*ET* 152); *Reden*[2], pp. 96–97 (*ET* 74); *Reden*[1], p. 10 (*ET* 7).

[23] *Reden*[1], p. 207 (*ET* 171); *Der christliche Glaube*, II, 135–136.

[24] *Reden*[1], p. 3 (*ET* 2); *Reden*[2], p. 92 (*ET* 70); *Reden*[1], p. 165 (*ET* 134); p. 163 (*ET* 131–132); p. 97 (*ET* 75); *Reden*[3], p. 190 (*ET* 156).

[25] *Reden*[3], p. 118 (*ET* 91); *Reden*[1], p. 152 (*ET* 123); *Reden*[3], p. 176 (*ET* 143); *Reden*[1], p. 208 (*ET* 172); *Reden*[2], p. 56 (*ET* 44). My discussion of this entire problem has been shaped by the essays of Joachim Wach, *Meister und Jünger: Zwei religionsgeschichtliche Betrachtungen* (Tübingen, 1925).

[26] Cf. Augustine, *The Teacher* (*De magistro*), XI, 36–38, ed. Joseph M. Colleran (Westminster, Md., 1950), pp. 175–177; Reidar Thomte, *Kierkegaard's Philosophy of Religion* (Princeton, 1948), pp. 200–203. *Reden*[2], p. 91 (*ET* 70); *Reden*[1], pp. 281–287 (*ET* 245–250); *Reden*[2], p. 285 (*ET* 248).

[27] *Reden*[1], p. 259 (*ET* 225); *Reden*[2], p. 261 (*ET* 227).

[28] On Judas Iscariot, cf. the excursus of Karl Barth, *Church Dogmatics,* II : 2, eds. G. W. Bromiley and T. F. Torrance (Edinburgh, 1957), 458–506. The catalogue of accusations is in *Sendschreiben an Lücke,* p. 19. Cf. *Reden*[1], p. 52 (*ET* 40); p. 172 (*ET* 139); *Reden*[2], p. 286 (*ET* 249). See Karl Barth, *Protestant Thought: From Rousseau to Ritschl,* tr. Brian Cozens, intro. by Jaroslav Pelikan (New York, 1959), p. 311.

[29] *Reden*[1], p. 116 (*ET* 89); *Reden*[2], p. 117 (*ET* 90); p. 65 (*ET* 54); *Reden*[1], p. 239 (*ET* 211); *Reden*[3], p. 258 (*ET* 224).

[30] Karl Barth, *Protestant Thought,* p. 327 (my own tr.).

[31] Francis Bacon, *Of the Proficience and Advancement of Learning Divine and Human,* Book Two, chapter V, paragraph 2.

[32] Jaroslav Pelikan, *Obedient Rebels: Catholic Substance and Protestant Principle in Luther's Reformation* (New York, 1964), pp. 19 ff., 204 ff.

Chapter II The Challenge to Creation

[1] Schleiermacher, *Der christliche Glaube,* I, 195–198. In fact, Schleiermacher's own view of *Heilsgeschichte* had much in common with an evolutionary conception of history.

[2] Cf., for example, Kenneth K. Bailey, *Southern White Protestantism in the Twentieth Century* (New York, 1964), pp. 72–91.

[3] See Werner Elert, *The Structure of Lutheranism,* I, tr. Walter A. Hansen, foreword Jaroslav Pelikan (St. Louis, 1962), 418–431, setting straight many of the secondary accounts.

[4] Arthur O. Lovejoy, "The Principle of Plenitude and the New

Cosmography," *The Great Chain of Being: A Study of the History of an Idea* (New York, 1960), pp. 99–143.

[5] William Paley, *View of the Evidences of Christianity* (1794), ed. Richard Whateley (London, 1953).

[6] In 1655 Isaac de la Peyrère published his *Praeadamitae,* thus precipitating a controversy over polygenism; cf. Hans Joachim Schoeps, *Philosemitismus im Barock: Religions- und geistesgeschichtliche Untersuchungen* (Tübingen, 1952), pp. 3–18.

[7] The nearest thing to such a history is the learned book of Otto Zöckler, *Geschichte der Beziehungen zwischen Theologie und Naturwissenschaft, mit besonderer Rücksicht auf Schöpfungsgeschichte,* 2 vols. (Gütersloh, 1877–1879); Zöckler was an Old Testament scholar, and therefore his monograph is an extended chapter in the history of exegesis.

[8] Gerhard von Rad, *Genesis: A Commentary,* tr. John H. Marks (Philadelphia, 1961), pp. 42–65.

[9] Werner Foerster, s. v. "ktizo etc.," *Theologisches Wörterbuch zum Neuen Testament,* ed. Gerhard Kittel (Stuttgart, 1938 ff.), III, 1004.

[10] Ibid., pp. 1027–1034.

[11] Cf. Rudolf Bultmann, *Theologie des Neuen Testaments* (Tübingen, 1953), pp. 222–228.

[12] Emil Brunner. *Man in Revolt: A Christian Anthropology,* tr. Olive Wyon (Philadelphia, 1947), pp. 82–113.

[13] Justin Martyr, *Apology,* I, 59.

[14] Aristides, *Apology,* in John of Damascus, *Barlaam and Ioasaph,* XXVII, 239.

[15] Tatian, *Address to the Greeks,* 5; cf. Jaroslav Pelikan, *The Shape of Death: Life, Death, and Immortality in the Early Fathers* (New York and Nashville, 1961), pp. 11–29.

[16] See the passages collected in E. F. Osborn, *The Philosophy of Clement of Alexandria* (Cambridge, 1957), p. 33.

[17] Theophilus, *Ad Autolycum,* II, 10.

[18] Tertullian, *The Treatise Against Hermogenes,* 21, 4.

[19] Tertullian, *Against Marcion,* I, 20.

[20] Ibid., IV, 14.

[21] Cf. Richard McKeon, "Aristotelianism in Western Christianity," *Environmental Factors in Christian History,* eds. John Thomas McNeill et al. (Chicago, 1939), pp. 221–223, on the eternity of the world.

[22] Thomas Aquinas, *Summa Theologica,* I, Q. 2, Art. 3.

[23] Ibid., Q. 45, Art. 1.

[24] Thomas Aquinas, *Treatise on Separate Substances,* ed. Francis J. Lescoe (West Hartford, 1963), Ch. XV, No. 84, p. 128.

[25] *Lectures on Genesis, WA* 42, 57 (*LW* 1, 75).

[26] See p. 65.

[27] Johann Quenstedt, *Theologia Didactico-Polemica* (1685), in *The Doctrinal Theology of the Evangelical Lutheran Church,* ed. Heinrich Schmid, tr. Charles A. Hay and Henry E. Jacobs (Philadelphia, 1889), p. 179.

[28] Cf. Jaroslav Pelikan, *Luther the Expositor: Introduction to the Reformer's Exegetical Writings* (St. Louis, 1959), pp. 237–254.

Chapter III Creation as History

[1] The Latin text of the *Enarratio in Genesin* appears in *WA* 42–44; it will occupy Vols. 1–8 of *LW,* five of which (1–4 and 7) have now appeared.

[2] Cf. *Luther the Expositor,* pp. 89–109.

[3] See Peter Meinhold, *Die Genesisvorlesung Luthers und ihre Herausgeber* (Stuttgart, 1936), and my comments, LW 1, xi–xii.

[4] *WA* 42, 99 (*LW* 1, 132); *WA* 42, 138 (*LW* 1, 185); *WA* 42, 173 (*LW* 1, 233); *WA* 42, 367 (*LW* 2, 150).

[5] See the brief comments of Michael Reu, *Luther and the Scriptures* (Columbus, 1944), pp. 103–108.

[6] *WA* 42, 219 (*LW* 1, 298); *WA* 42, 272 (*LW* 2, 15, and my note there).

[7] On Augustine and Hilary, *WA* 42, 4 (*LW* 1, 4, and my notes there); *WA* 42, 91 (*LW* 1, 121); *WA* 42, 62 (*LW* 1, 82).

[8] *WA* 42, 99 (*LW* 1, 132); *WA* 42, 315 (*LW* 2, 74).

[9] *WA* 42, 309 (*LW* 2, 67); *WA* 42, 230 (*LW* 1, 313).

[10] Mircea Eliade, *Myths, Dreams, and Mysteries,* tr. Philip Mairet (New York, 1960), p. 55.

[11] Cf. Anders Nygren, *Agape and Eros,* tr. Philip S. Watson (Philadelphia, 1953), pp. 681–691.

[12] *WA* 42, 78 (*LW* 1, 102); *WA* 42, 54 (*LW* 1, 72); *WA* 42, 79 (*LW* 1, 104); *WA* 42, 100 (*LW* 1, 133); *WA* 42, 162 (LW 1, 217); *WA* 42, 55 (*LW* 1, 72); *WA* 42, 425 (*LW* 2, 231); *WA* 42, 76 (*LW* 1, 100); *WA* 42, 46 (*LW* 1, 62, and my note there); *WA* 42, 70 (*LW* 1, 92).

[13] *WA* 42, 96 (*LW* 1, 128).

[14] *WA* 42, 79 (*LW* 1, 104); cf. George W. Forell, *Faith Active in Love* (New York, 1954), pp. 139–155.

[15] *WA* 42, 49 (*LW* 1, 66).

[16] *WA* 42, 79 (*LW* 1, 105); *WA* 42, 102 (*LW* 1, 136); *WA* 42, 89 (*LW* 1, 117); *WA* 42, 105 (*LW* 1, 139).

[17] *WA* 42, 84 (*LW* 1, 111).

[18] On Irenaeus, cf. *The Shape of Death,* p. 103; also Paul Tillich, *Systematic Theology,* II (Chicago, 1957), 33 ff.

[19] *The Shape of Death,* pp. 107–109.

[20] *WA* 42, 97 (*LW* 1, 130).

[21] *WA* 42, 48 (*LW* 1, 64); *WA* 42, 58 (*LW* 1, 76); *WA* 42, 114 (*LW* 1, 151); *WA* 42, 315 (*LW* 2, 74); *WA* 42, 152 (*LW* 1, 204); *WA* 42, 156 (*LW* 1, 208); *WA* 42, 99 (*LW* 1, 133).

[22] Cf. Jaroslav Pelikan, "Paul Tillich und die dogmatische Tradition," *Gott Ist am Werk: Festschrift für Landesbischof D. Hanns Lilje,* ed. Heinz Brunotte (Hamburg, 1959), pp. 28–31.

[23] *WA* 42, 214 (*LW* 1, 290); *WA* 42, 54 (*LW* 1, 71).

[24] *WA* 42, 31 (*LW* 1, 41); *WA* 42, 36 (*LW* 1, 48). See the excellent summary by John Dillenberger, *Protestant Thought and Natural Science* (New York, 1960), pp. 21–49.

[25] Cf. E. G. Schwiebert, *Luther and His Times: The Reformation from a New Perspective* (St. Louis, 1950), pp. 608–612.

[26] Andrew Dickson White, *A History of the Warfare of Science with Theology in Christendom* (New York, 1925), is a fascinating combination of insight and myopia, combining historical data available nowhere else with judgments that are based, quite frankly, on the author's personal presuppositions.

[27] Carl Friedrich Weizsäcker, *The History of Nature*, tr. Fred D. Wieck (Chicago, 1949); Karl Heim, *Christian Faith and Natural Science,* tr. N. Horton Smith (New York, 1953).

Chapter IV The Doctrine of Creation

[1] Cf. Edmund Schlink, *The Theology of the Lutheran Confessions,* tr. Paul F. Koehneke and Herbert J. A. Bouman (Philadelphia, 1961), pp. 37–66.

[2] See p. 84.

[3] See p. 135, note 22.

[4] Thomas Aquinas, *Summa Theologica,* I, Q. 46.

[5] Ibid., Q. 32, Art. 1; instructive in this connection are the remarks of Mark Pontifex, *Belief in the Trinity* (New York, 1954), pp. 68–70.

[6] A stimulating discussion of this problem is H. E. Eisenhuth, *Ontologie and Theologie* (Göttingen, 1933).

[7] Cf. *Obedient Rebels,* p. 46, n.2.

[8] Formula of Concord, Solid Declaration, VIII, 18, *Bek.* 1022 (*BC* 594); and Catalog of Testimonies, I, *Bek.* 1104–1105.

[9] Cf. the stirring analysis of Johann Haar, *Initium creaturae Dei* (Gütersloh, 1939), especially pp. 13–27.

[10] See Jaroslav Pelikan, "The Relation of Faith and Knowledge in the Lutheran Confessions," *Concordia Theological Monthly,* XXI (1950), 321–331.

[11] "I have had so many experiences of the divinity of Christ that I must say: Either there is no God or he is it," *WA Ti* 1, 269.

[12] Wilhelm Lütgert, *Schöpfung und Offenbarung: Eine Theologie des ersten Artikels* (Gütersloh, 1934), p. 27.

[13] Max Lackmann, *Vom Geheimnis der Schöpfung* (Stuttgart, 1952), e.g., pp. 272–273. Lackmann's study is basically a history of the exegesis of Romans 1 : 18–23, 2 : 14–16, Acts 14 : 15–17, and 17 : 22–29, from the second century to the beginnings of Protestant Orthodoxy.

[14] Elert, op. cit., pp. 49–58.

[15] Formula of Concord, Solid Declaration, IX, 53, *Bek.* 1079 (*BC* 625).

[16] The German phrase is *sampt allen Kreaturn,* the Latin *una cum omnibus creaturis,* Small Catechism, II, 2, *Bek.* 510 (*BC* 345).

[17] Thus Brunner's discussion of "Man in the Cosmos," op. cit., pp. 409–434, seems to be informed by certain idealistic presuppositions.

[18] Apology of the Augsburg Confession, II, 18, *Bek.* 150 (*BC* 102–103).

[19] Formula of Concord, Solid Declaration, I, 34, *Bek.* 855 (*BC* 514).

[20] Large Catechism, I, 26, *Bek.* 566 (*BC* 368).

[21] For some suggestions about the history of the exegesis of Exodus 3 : 14, cf. *Luther the Expositor,* pp. 24–27.

[22] Apology of the Augsburg Confession, XVI, 6, *Bek.* 309 (*BC* 223).

[23] Ibid., VII, 50, *Bek.* 246 (*BC* 178).

[24] Eduard Schweizer, *Ego Eimi* (Göttingen, 1939), pp. 124–167; on "I am the light," especially pp. 161–166.

[25] Formula of Concord, Solid Declaration, VII, 44, *Bek.* 985 (*BC* 577).

[26] Formula of Concord, Solid Declaration, XII, 25, *Bek.* 1096 (*BC* 635).

[27] Ibid., par. 28, *Bek.* 1097 (*BC* 635).

[28] Formula of Concord, Solid Declaration, I, 43, *Bek.* 857 (*BC* 516).

[29] Cf. Martin Chemnitz, *De duabus naturis in Christo* (Leipzig, 1580), pp. 33–35.

[30] Formula of Concord, Solid Declaration, III, 57, *Bek.* 934 (*BC* 549–550).

[31] Formula of Concord, Solid Declaration, VIII, 70, *Bek.* 1040 (*BC* 605).

Chapter V The Mystery of the Known

[1] *Lectures on Genesis, WA* 42, 322 (*LW* 2, 86).

[2] Ibid., *WA* 43, 336 (*LW* 4, 279).

[3] Thus, for example, in his exegesis of Genesis 15 : 13–16, *Lectures on Genesis, WA* 42, 574 (*LW* 3, 36); or in his exposition of Psalm 90 : 2, *Commentary on Psalm 90, WA* 40–III, 512 (*LW* 13, 93). Cf. Brunner, *Man in Revolt,* pp. 89–91; and Paul Tillich, *The Shaking of the Foundations* (New York, 1948), pp. 38–51.

[4] *Commentary on Psalm 112, WA* 19, 316 (*LW* 13, 404–405).

[5] *Commentary on the Sermon on the Mount, WA* 32, 325 (*LW* 21, 37).

[6] Cf. Ragnar Bring, *Dualismen hos Luther* (Lund, 1929), p. 23 and passim.

[7] Cf. *Obedient Rebels,* p. 45, n.1.

[8] Cf. pp. 93–94.

[9] On Luther's experience of the *mysterium tremendum et fascinans,* see Rudolf Otto, *The Idea of the Holy,* tr. John W. Harvey (London, 1946), pp. 97–112.

[10] Cf. Mircea Eliade, *Cosmos and History: The Myth of the Eternal Return,* tr. Willard R. Trask (New York, 1959), pp. 97–112.

[11] See pp. 39–40.

[12] *Lectures on the Minor Prophets, WA* 13, 440; cf. *Luther the Expositor,* pp. 58–59.

[13] G. van der Leeuw, *Religion in Essence and Manifestation,* tr. J. E. Turner (New York, 1963), II, 435–446.

[14] George H. Williams, *Wilderness and Paradise in Christian Thought* (New York, 1962).

[15] Shirley Jackson Case, *The Origins of Christian Supernaturalism* (Chicago, 1946), p. 1.

[16] *The Bondage of the Will, WA* 18, 614–618.

[17] Cf. *Sermons on the Gospel of St. John, WA* 46, (*LW* 22, 200–202).

[18] See Luther's comments, *Lectures on Genesis, WA* 42, 179 (*LW* 1, 241).

[19] *How Christians Should Regard Moses, WA* 24, 12–13 (*LW* 35, 171–172); cf. *From Luther to Kierkegaard,* p. 18.

[20] Small Catechism, II, 2, *Bek.* 510 (*BC* 345); Large Catechism, II, 13, *Bek.* 648 (*BC* 412).

[21] *Lectures on Genesis, WA* 44, 374–375 (*LW* 7, 100–101).

[22] *Commentary on Isaiah 53, WA* 40–III, 685–746.

[23] *Commentary on Psalm 8* (*LW* 12, 118).

[24] *Preface to the Prophets* (*LW* 35, 276).

[25] The Masoretic text reads *heqitsothi,* but it has been suggested that *haqitsothi* would be a preferable reading.

[26] Jaroslav Pelikan, *The Light of the World: A Basic Image in Early Christian Thought* (New York, 1962), pp. 103–107; *The Shape of Death,* pp. 55–73.

Chapter VI The Doctrine of Man

[1] Formula of Concord, Solid Declaration, II, 2, *Bek.* 870–871 (*BC* 520); the distinction is based on Peter Lombard, *Sentences,* II, dist. 25, ch. 6.

[2] Smalcald Articles, III, i, 3, *Bek.* 434 (*BC* 302).

[3] See p. 138, note 16.

[4] This thought, based on Lev. 26 : 36, occurs often in Luther, e.g., *Lectures on Genesis, WA* 42, 127 (*LW* 1, 170–171).

[5] Bultmann, *Theologie des Neuen Testaments,* pp. 344–345.

[6] Large Catechism, II, 13, *Bek.* 648 (*BC* 412); Small Catechism, II, 2, *Bek.* 510 (*BC* 345).

[7] Formula of Concord, Solid Declaration, I, 36, *Bek.* 855 (*BC* 514).

[8] On the theological validity of the idea of *imago Dei,* see the remarks of Friedrich Karl Schumann, "Imago Dei," in *Imago Dei: Beiträge zur theologischen Anthropologie,* ed. Heinrich Bornkamm (Giessen, 1932), pp. 167–180.

[9] Cf. Heiko A. Oberman, *The Harvest of Medieval Theology: Gabriel Biel and Late Medieval Nominalism* (Cambridge, Mass., 1963), pp. 66–67.

[10] Apology of the Augsburg Confession, II, 18, *Bek.* 150 (*BC* 102–103).

[11] Ibid., par. 16–17, *Bek.* 150 (*BC* 102).

[12] See, for example, Tileman Hesshusius, *Examen theologicum* (2nd ed., Frankfort, 1578), p. 28, who defines the image of God as "a light and wisdom in the mind." Martin Chemnitz, on the other hand, saw it "in the whole mind, whole heart, whole will, and in all the members of the body and powers of the soul," *Examen Concilii*

Tridentini (1565–1573), ed. E. Preuss (Leipzig, 1915), p. 103. See also Matthias Hafenreffer, *Loci theologici* (2nd ed., Tübingen, 1601), pp. 72–78, where *imago Dei* follows a discussion of immortality.

[13] Formula of Concord, Solid Declaration, I, 10, *Bek.* 848 (*BC* 510).

[14] Apology of the Augsburg Confession, II, 19, *Bek.* 150–151 (*BC* 103).

[15] Cf. the discussion of "Sin as a Religious Concept" in Gustaf Aulén, *The Faith of the Christian Church,* tr. Eric H. Wahlstrom and G. Everett Arden (Philadelphia, 1948), pp. 260–261.

[16] For the definition of original sin as "concupiscence materially but the privation of original righteousness formally," cf. Thomas Aquinas, *Summa Theologica,* I–II, Q. 82, Art. 3. It is interesting that although the distinction between the *formale* and the *materiale* of sin was scorned by the Apology of the Augsburg Confession, II, 4, *Bek.* 147 (*BC* 101), it soon returned to Reformation theology; cf., for one example, Johann Spangenberg, *Margarita theologica, continens praecipuos locos doctrinae Christianae* (Frankfort, 1557), pp. 20–21.

[17] Apology of the Augsburg Confession, II, 23, *Bek.* 151 (*BC* 103); on *carentia justitiae originalis,* see also Formula of Concord, Solid Declaration, I, 10, *Bek.* 848 (*BC* 510), and Spangenberg, op. cit., p. 19.

[18] Apology of the Augsburg Confession, II, 26, *Bek.* 152 (*BC* 103): cf. Wilhelm Braun, *Die Bedeutung der Concupiscenz in Luthers Leben und Lehre* (Berlin, 1908) for a complete discussion.

[19] *Man in Revolt,* pp. 169 ff.

[20] Lenhart Pinomaa, *Der Zorn Gottes in der Theologie Luthers* (Helsinki, 1938).

[21] Apology of the Augsburg Confession, IV, 36–40, *Bek.* 167 (*BC* 112); cf. Elert, *The Structure of Lutheranism,* pp. 17–58, on Reformation and post-Reformation developments.

[22] Apology of the Augsburg Confession, II, 46–50, *Bek.* 156–157 (*BC* 106).

[23] Formula of Concord, Solid Declaration, II, 11, *Bek.* 875 (*BC* 522).

[24] Cf. Günther Bornkamm, "Die Offenbarung des Zornes Gottes," *Zeitschrift für die neutestamentliche Wissenschaft,* XXXIV (1935–1936), 239–262.

[25] Formula of Concord, Solid Declaration, I, 8, *Bek.* 847 (*BC* 510), referring to passages both in the Smalcald Articles and in the Apology of the Augsburg Confession; also par. 60, *Bek.* 864–865 (*BC* 519).

[26] Formula of Concord, Solid Declaration, I, 54–62, *Bek.* 861–866

(*BC* 517–519); on the entire controversy that brought this forth, see Wilhelm Preger, *Matthias Flacius Illyricus und seine Zeit* (Erlangen, 1859–1861), II, 310–412.

[27] Formula of Concord, Solid Declaration, I, 34–47, *Bek.* 855–856 (*BC* 514).

[28] Ibid., par. 43–44, *Bek.* 857–858 (*BC* 515–516).

[29] On the latter alternative, cf. Martin Chemnitz, *De duabus naturis in Christo,* pp. 33–35.

[30] Formula of Concord, Solid Declaration, I, 29, *Bek.* 853 (*BC* 513).

[31] For a discussion of the basic problems in Augustine's doctrine of man, cf. Erich Dinkler, *Die Anthropologie Augustins* (Stuttgart, 1934).

[32] Thomas Aquinas, *Summa Theologica,* I–II, Q. 81, Art. 5; cf. Carlo Balić, "The Mediaeval Controversy over the Immaculate Conception up to the Death of Scotus," *The Dogma of the Immaculate Conception. History and Significance,* ed. Edward Dennis O'Connor (Notre Dame, 1958), pp. 188–197.

[33] A. F. C. Vilmar, *Die Augsburgische Confession* (Gütersloh, 1870), p. 51.

[34] Formula of Concord, Solid Declaration, I, 7, *Bek.* 847 (*BC* 510).

[35] Cf. Lorenzo Valla, "Dialogue on Free Will," tr. Charles Edward Trinkaus, *The Renaissance Philosophy of Man, eds.* Ernst Cassirer et al. (Chicago, 1948), pp. 155–182.

[36] *The Bondage of the Will, WA* 18, 618, 718, 786; cf. Rudolf Hermann, *Zu Luthers Lehre vom unfreien Willen* (Berlin and Leipzig, 1931).

[37] See the summaries of Melanchthon's development in Hans Engelland, *Melanchthon, Glauben und Handeln* (Munich, 1931), pp. 80–90, 237–258, with full source references.

[38] Preger, op. cit., II, 212–214.

[39] On this parallel, see the interesting comments about Flacius in Barth, *Kirchliche Dogmatik,* III : 2, 29–32.

[40] Formula of Concord, Solid Declaration, II, 9, *Bek.* 874 (*BC* 521).

[41] Jaroslav Pelikan, "Natural Theology in David Hollaz," *Concordia Theological Monthly,* XVIII (1947), 253–263; and the briefer summary, *From Luther to Kierkegaard,* pp. 65–69.

[42] Augsburg Confession, XVIII, 1, *Bek.* 73 (*BC* 39). Cf. the exposition of Jacob Heerbrand, *Compendium theologiae* (Wittenberg, 1582), pp. 224–232; it is significant, in connection with the

trend described in note 12 above, that Heerbrand equates *arbitrium* with *intellectus, mens vel ratio,* p. 224.

[43] Apology of the Augsburg Confession, IV, 14, *Bek.* 161–162 (*BC* 109).

[44] Ibid., par. 22–24, *Bek.* 164–165 (*BC* 110).

[45] Ibid., par. 303, *Bek.* 219 (*BC* 154).

[46] Formula of Concord, Solid Declaration, II, 24, *Bek.* 882 (*BC* 525–526).

[47] Formula of Concord, Epitome, II, 17, *Bek.* 780 (*BC* 472).

[48] The classic exposition of this dictum is that of Rudolf Hermann, *Luthers These 'Gerecht und Sünder zugleich'* (Gütersloh, 1930). Also of great value is the work of Erdmann Schott, *Fleisch und Geist nach Luthers Lehre* (Leipzig, 1928).

[49] Cf. Aegidius Hunnius, *Articulus de justificatione hominis* (Frankfort, 1590), pp. 19–20, p. 63, on imputation.

[50] See the summary of the entire development in Otto Ritschl, *Dogmengeschichte des Protestantismus,* II : 1 (Leipzig, 1912), 455–500.

[51] Apology of the Augsburg Confession, IV, 72, *Bek.* 174 (*BC* 117). From the voluminous literature of the discussion on this passage, which began with Friedrich Loofs, I cite only two works, which summarize the preceding debates: Carl Stange, "Ueber eine Stelle in der Apologie: Ein Beitrag zur Rechtfertigungslehre der Apologie," in his *Theologische Aufsätze* (Leipzig, 1905), pp. 50–73; and Engelland, op. cit., pp. 541 ff.

[52] Lowell C. Green, *Die Entwicklung der evangelischen Rechtfertigungslehre bei Melanchthon bis 1521 im Vergleich mit der Luthers* (Erlangen, 1955), is an effort to reorient the discussion of Melanchthon's doctrine.

[53] Formula of Concord, Solid Declaration, III, 54–56, *Bek.* 932–934 (*BC* 548–549).

[54] Apology of the Augsburg Confession, II, 35–37, *Bek.* 153–154 (*BC* 104–105); cf. Chemnitz, *Examen,* pp. 105–107.

[55] Formula of Concord, Epitome, XI, 9, *Bek.* 818 (*BC* 495).

[56] Schott, op. cit., pp. 54–56.

[57] Apology of the Augsburg Confession, IV, 189–193, *Bek.* 197–198 (*BC* 133).

[58] Ibid., Art. VII, 18, *Bek.,* 237 (*BC* 171).

[59] Formula of Concord, Solid Declaration, II, 68, *Bek.* 899 (*BC* 534).

[60] Ibid., Art. XI, 28, *Bek.* 1071–1072 (*BC* 620–621).

Chapter VII Divine Justification and Human Justice

[1] Unless otherwise indicated, all references in this chapter will be to my new translation of the *Lectures on Galatians, LW* 26–27. On the relation of these *Lectures* to Luther's earlier exposition of the epistle, see the study of Karin Bornkamm, *Luthers Auslegungen des Galaterbriefs von 1519 und 1531: Ein Vergleich* (Berlin, 1963).

[2] *WA* 40–I, 337 (*LW* 26, 208–209).

[3] *WA* 40–I, 43–45 (*LW* 26, 6–7).

[4] Thus Christ is also "the fulfillment of the law" (*WA* 40–I, 501; *LW* 26, 324), "the propitiator for the sins of the whole world" (*WA* 40–I, 91; *LW* 26, 37), the one who "expiated [sin] by his death" (*WA* 40–II, 95; *LW* 27, 76).

[5] *WA* 40–I, 278–279 (*LW* 26, 164).

[6] *WA* 40–I, 567 (*LW* 26, 371).

[7] *WA* 40–I, 569 (*LW* 26, 373).

[8] *WA* 40–I, 554 (*LW* 26, 362–363).

[9] *WA* 40–I, 226 (*LW* 26, 128).

[10] *WA* 40–I, 228 (*LW* 26, 129).

[11] *WA* 40–I, 551 (*LW* 26, 361).

[12] *WA* 40–II, 147 (*LW* 27, 115–116).

[13] *WA* 40–I, 368 (*LW* 26, 232); see pp. 90–91.

[14] *WA* 40–I, 369 (*LW* 26, 233).

[15] *WA* 40–I, 368 (*LW* 26, 232).

[16] *WA* 40–I, 226 (*LW* 26, 127–128).

[17] Cf. *Lectures on Genesis, WA* 43, 198 (*LW* 4, 87, and my note there).

[18] *WA* 40–II, 142 (*LW* 27, 111).

[19] *WA* 40–I, 410 (*LW* 26, 262).

[20] *WA* 40–I, 292 (*LW* 26, 173).

[21] Cf. Heiko A. Oberman, "Facientibus quod in se est Deus non denegat gratiam," *Harvard Theological Review,* LV (1962), 317–342.

[22] *WA* 40–I, 292 (*LW* 26, 173–174).

[23] *WA* 40–I, 532 (*LW* 26, 347).

[24] *WA* 40–I, 615 (*LW* 26, 405).

[25] *WA* 40–I, 482 (*LW* 26, 310).

[26] *WA* 40–I, 590 (*LW* 26, 387).

[27] *WA* 40–I, 676 (*LW* 26, 450).

[28] *WA* 40–I, 619 (*LW* 26, 407).

[29] *WA* 40–I, 178 (*LW* 26, 97).

[30] *WA* 40–I, 673–674 (*LW* 26, 448).

[31] See the treatise of 1525, *How Christians Should Regard Moses*, *WA* 16, 363–393 (*LW* 35, 161–174).

[32] *WA* 40–I, 543 (*LW* 26, 354).

[33] Brian A. Gerrish, *Grace and Reason: A Study of the Theology of Luther* (Oxford, 1962), puts this issue into context.

[34] Aristotle, *Nicomachean Ethics,* III, 6–9.

[35] *WA* 40–II, 27 (*LW* 27, 23).

[36] The standard discussion is still that of Karl Holl, "Luther und das landesherrliche Kirchenregiment," *Gesammelte Aufsätze zur Kirchengeschichte, Vol. I: Luther* (7th ed., Tübingen, 1948), pp. 326–380.

[37] Thus Werner Elert, one of the ablest defenders of Luther's Reformation, conceded (writing in 1932) that "it is undeniable that [in Luther's thought] there lies the danger of an exaggeration of the role and authority of the state," *Morphologie des Luthertums, Vol. II: Soziallehren und Sozialwirkungen* (Munich, 1932), p. 333.

[38] *WA* 40–II, 26 (*LW* 27, 22).

[39] *WA* 40–I, 292 (*LW* 26, 173).

[40] *WA* 40–I, 306 (*LW* 26, 183).

[41] *WA* 40–I, 557 (*LW* 26, 364).

[42] *WA* 40–II, 25 (*LW* 27, 22).

[43] *WA* 40–II, 178 (*LW* 27, 139).

[44] *WA* 40–I, 570 (*LW* 26, 373).

[45] *Lectures on Genesis, WA* 44, 493 (*LW* 7, 261).

[46] Cf. Thomas Aquinas, *Summa Theologica,* I, Q. 1, Art. 8.

CHAPTER VIII THE THEOLOGIAN AS A HUMANISTIC SCHOLAR

[1] Heinrich Bornkamm, *Luther und das Alte Testament* (Tübingen, 1948), p. 6.

[2] Cf. Roland H. Bainton, *Yale and the Ministry: A History of Education for the Christian Ministry at Yale from the Founding in 1701* (New York, 1957), pp. 7–8 and passim.

[3] See the comments of Robert Maynard Hutchins, *The Higher Learning in America* (New Haven, 1936), pp. 98–109.

[4] Friedrich Schleiermacher, "Gelegentliche Gedanken über Universitäten in deutschem Sinn" (1808), in *Pädagogische Schriften*, edd. Theodor Schulz and Erich Weniger (Düsseldorf, 1957), II, 81–139; Adolf Harnack, "Die Bedeutung der theologischen Fakultäten," in *Erforschtes und Erlebtes* (Giessen, 1923), pp. 199–217; also Adolf Harnack, "Die Aufgabe der theologischen Fakultäten und die

allgemeine Religionsgeschichte, nebst einem Nachwort" (1901), in *Reden und Aufsätze,* II (Giessen, 1904), 161–187.

[5] See the essay on "A Faith for These Times" in Nathan M. Pusey, *The Age of the Scholar: Observations on Education in a Troubled Decade* (New York, 1964), pp. 1–8.

[6] See p. 133, note 11.

[7] Cf. Jaroslav Pelikan, "Introduction" to Adolf Harnack, *The Mission and Expansion of Christianity in the First Three Centuries,* tr. James Moffatt (new ed., New York, 1961).

[8] Ernest Renan, *Life of Jesus* (Modern Library translation; New York, 1927), p. 65.

[9] Cf. Edwin Arthur Burtt, *The Metaphysical Foundations of Modern Physical Science* (rev. ed., New York, 1954), pp. 220–226.

[10] See the observations of Benedetto Croce, *History: Its Theory and Practice,* tr. Douglas Ainslie (New York, 1960), pp. 292 ff.

[11] G. P. Gooch, *History and Historians in the Nineteenth Century* (2nd ed., Boston, 1959), pp. 72–121.

[12] Cf. Ferdinand Christian Baur, *Die Epochen der kirchlichen Geschichtsschreibung* (1852; Hildesheim, 1962), pp. 39–107; Harry Elmer Barnes, *A History of Historical Writing* (2nd ed., New York, 1962), pp. 121–135.

[13] See the fine summary by Wilhelm Pauck, "The Roman Catholic Critique of Protestantism," *The Heritage of the Reformation* (2nd ed., Glencoe, Ill., 1961), pp. 231 ff.

[14] R. G. Collingwood, *The Idea of History* (New York, 1956); Croce, op. cit.; C. N. Cochrane, *Thucydides and the Science of History* (London, 1929); Wilhelm Dilthey, *Pattern and Meaning in History,* ed. H. P. Rickman (New York, 1962).

[15] From a letter of Adolf Harnack to Martin Rade, January 1, 1929, referring to the theology of Karl Barth, cited in Agnes von Zahn-Harnack, *Adolf von Harnack* (2nd ed., Berlin, 1951), p. 416.

[16] In general, see Vincent A. Dearing, *A Manual of Textual Analysis* (Berkeley, 1959); Bruce M. Metzger, *The Text of the New Testament: Its Transmission, Corruption, and Restoration* (New York, 1964), pp. 95 ff.

[17] Cf. John Christian Burk, *A Memoir of the Life and Writings of John Albrecht Bengel,* tr. Robert Francis Walker (London, 1842), pp. 224–250.

[18] Anders Nygren, "The Role of the Self-Evident in History," *Journal of Religion,* XXVIII (1948), 235–241.

[19] See Collingwood, op. cit., pp. 205–334.

[20] See both the Foreword of 1933 and the Preface of 1959 by the

late Perry Miller to his *Orthodoxy in Massachuetts 1630–1650* (2nd ed., Boston, 1959), pp. xi–xxi, describing the origins of modern Puritan study.

[21] Cf. Charles Augustus Briggs, *History of the Study of Theology* (New York, 1916), II, 82–142, on Renaissance and Reformation.

[22] Sidney E. Mead, "The Rise of the Evangelical Conception of the Ministry in America 1607–1850," *The Ministry in Historical Perspectives,* eds. H. Richard Niebuhr and Daniel Day Williams (New York, 1956), pp. 207–249.

[23] H. Richard Niebuhr, Daniel Day Williams, and James M. Gustafson, *The Advancement of Theological Education* (New York, 1957), pp. 1–26.

[24] *Commentary on Psalm 82, WA* 21–I, 211 (*LW* 13, 65).

[25] "By the grace of God, we are holy apostates," *Lectures on Genesis, WA* 42, 412 (*LW* 2, 213).

Chapter IX The Church and the Christian Intellectual

[1] Ignatius of Antioch, Ephesians 18 : 1, tr. James A. Kleist, *The Epistles of St. Clement of Rome and St. Ignatius of Antioch* (Westminster, Md., 1946), pp. 66–67.

[2] Cf. Henri de Lubac, *Histoire et esprit: L'intelligence de l'Écriture d'après Origène* (Paris, 1959), pp. 83–86; and the criticisms of his position in R. P. C. Hanson, *Allegory and Event: A Study of the Sources and Significance of Origen's Interpretation of Scripture* (Richmond, Va., 1959), pp. 213–214.

[3] Alexis de Tocqueville, *Democracy in America,* ed. Phillips Bradley (New York, 1945), I, 55; cf. Joachim Wach, "The Rôle of Religion in the Social Philosophy of Alexis de Tocqueville," *Types of Religious Experience Christian and Non-Christian* (London, 1951), pp. 171–186.

[4] Guenter Lewy, *The Catholic Church and Nazi Germany* (New York, 1964); for a summary of recent studies on Protestantism under the Nazis, cf. Arthur C. Cochrane, *The Church's Confession under Hitler* (Philadelphia, 1962).

[5] See the concise statement in Pauck, *The Heritage of the Reformation,* pp. 207–208.

[6] Tocqueville, loc. cit.

[7] The pioneering studies were those of Karl Eger, *Die Anschauungen Luthers vom Beruf: Ein Beitrag zur Ethik Luthers* (Giessen, 1900); and Einar Billing, *Our Calling* (1909), tr. Conrad Bergendoff (Rock Island, Ill., 1952).

[8] From a quite different quarter some of these same implications have been drawn by Karl Rahner, *Theology for Renewal: Bishops, Priests, Laity,* tr. Cecily Hastings and Richard Strachan (New York, 1964), pp. 85–93.

[9] Cf. Irenaeus, *Against Heresies,* I, 8, 3.

[10] *Ibid.,* I, 10, 3.

[11] The comments of Karl Rahner, op cit., pp. 123–125, are appropriate here.

[12] See the sobering discussion of "The Perplexed Profession" in H. Richard Niebuhr, *The Purpose of the Church and Its Ministry: Reflections on the Aims of Theological Education* (New York, 1956), pp. 48 ff.

[13] Pauck, *Heritage of the Reformation,* p. 117.

[14] Cf. Martin E. Marty, *The New Shape of American Religion* (New York, 1959), pp. 122 ff.; *Second Chance for American Protestants* (New York, 1963), pp. 137 ff.

[15] On the problem of "spiritual authority," cf. H. Richard Niebuhr, *The Purpose of the Church and Its Ministry,* p. 89.

[16] The Westminster Shorter Catechism (1647), *Creeds of Christendom,* ed. Philip Schaff (New York, 1919), III, 676.

[17] Cf. Heinrich Scholz, "Fruitio Dei: Ein Beitrag zur Geschichte der Theologie und der Mystik," *Glaube und Unglaube in der Weltgeschichte: Ein Kommentar zu Augustins De civitate Dei* (Leipzig, 1911), pp. 197–235.

[18] *A Sincere Admonition by Martin Luther to All Christians to Guard Against Insurrection and Rebellion, WA* 8, 685 (*LW* 45, 70).

[19] See pp. 98–99.

[20] See pp. 30–31.

[21] See pp. 101–102.

[22] Gilbert K. Chesterton, *Orthodoxy* (Image Books ed., New York, 1959), pp. 79–80.

Index